BASIC INSTRUCTOR
GUITAR VOL. 1
JERRY SNYDER

This course is designed for individual or group instruction. Volume 1 is divided into two sections: Section One focuses on chords, theory, accompaniment, and songs; Section Two focuses on notation, music fundamentals, solos, and ensembles. The material be more difficult in both sections and should be learne

Alfred
Alfred Music
16320 Roscoe Blvd., Suite 100
P.O. Box 10003
Van Nuys, CA 91410-0003
alfred.com

Third Edition

Cover Photos:
Classical guitar by Richard Bruné.
Fender Stratocaster courtesy of Fender Musical Instruments, Inc.
Martin D-16 acoustic courtesy of the Martin Guitar Company.

Book ISBN-10: 0-7390-5849-5
ISBN-13: 978-0-7390-5849-7

Book & CD ISBN-10: 0-7390-5851-7
ISBN-13: 978-0-7390-5851-0

CD ISBN-10: 0-7390-5850-9
ISBN-13: 978-0-7390-5850-3

TYPES OF GUITARS

Broadly speaking, there are two types of guitars: *steel string* guitars and *nylon string* guitars. Either type may be *acoustic* (not amplified) or *electric* (amplified). The essential difference is in their *timbre*, or tone quality. The selection of a guitar is really a matter of personal choice.

Steel String Guitar

The steel string guitar is characterized by a rather narrow fingerboard, a pick guard, and steel strings. The flat-top steel string guitar is a good beginning guitar. The timbre, or tone color, is bright, brassy, and forceful, and lends itself to folk, country, ragtime, blues, and pop styles of music. This kind of guitar is most often played pickstyle, but fingerstyle technique is also commonly used. Light gauge strings may make depressing the strings easier. Never put nylon strings on a steel string guitar.

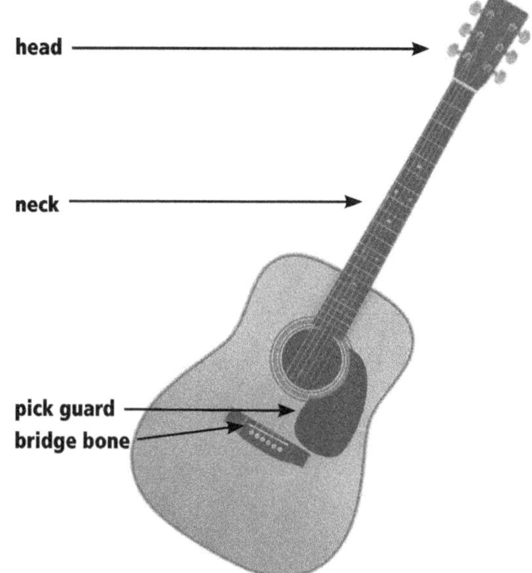

Nylon String Guitar

The nylon string (classical) guitar is characterized by a wide fingerboard, an open peg box (slotted tuning mechanism), and nylon strings. Some models have a slightly narrower neck than that of a traditional classical guitar. The nylon string guitar is an excellent guitar for the beginner, as the strings have less tension than those of a steel string guitar and are easy to depress. The timbre is dark, mellow, and delicate. This type of guitar has a rich repertoire of classical music and is also a popular choice for folk, Latin, and jazz. Picking hand fingerstyle techniques are generally used. Do not put steel strings on a nylon string guitar.

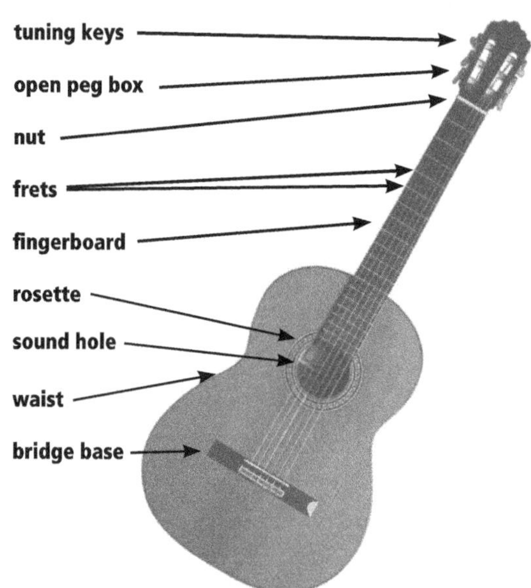

Electric Guitar

The *solid body* electric guitar is popular with rock, blues, and country musicians. The *semi-hollow* and *hollow body* electric guitars are popular choices for country, pop, blues, and jazz musical styles. These guitars have thin cut-away necks designed to enable the player to perform in high positions. Electric guitars have volume and tone controls that allow for a wide range of tone qualities ranging from bright to dark.

Without an amplifier, the electric guitar is very hard to hear. A 10-watt amplifier is adequate for practicing, and earphones that run on a 9-volt battery can be plugged directly into the guitar.

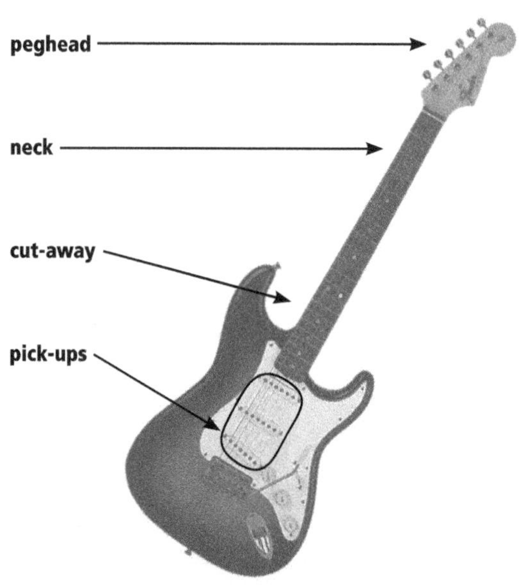

TUNING THE GUITAR

The difficulty of tuning the guitar lies in matching one musical pitch to another. You usually have the additional distraction of attempting to match the pitch of the guitar to a pitch of an instrument with a different timbre such as a piano, pitch pipe, or tuning fork, or even matching the pitch of an open guitar string to a fretted (depressed) string. It will take a while to develop the "sense of pitch" necessary for tuning your guitar; there are many fairly inexpensive electronic tuners you might consider purchasing to assist you.

Tuning to a Piano

When tuning the guitar to a piano, begin with the 6th string (low E). Sound the tone on the piano, and use your "tonal memory" to match the pitch of the open 6th string on the guitar. This may be accomplished by first purposely lowering the open 6th string below the desired pitch, and while plucking the string with your thumb or pick, slowly turn the appropriate tuning key with your fretting hand until you have matched the pitch. Tune each string in this manner.

Tuning the Guitar to Itself

To tune the guitar to itself, either estimate the pitch of the 6th string (low E) or use a tuning fork, and then follow the steps outlined below.

CD 1 = TUNING REFERENCE TRACK

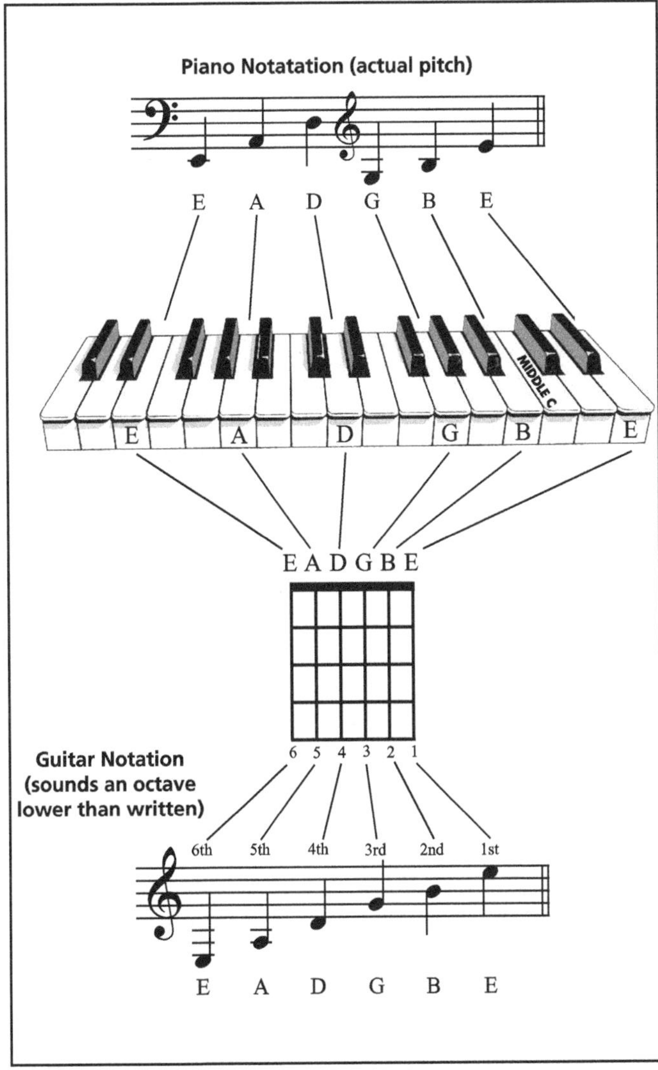

Tuning the guitar to a piano.

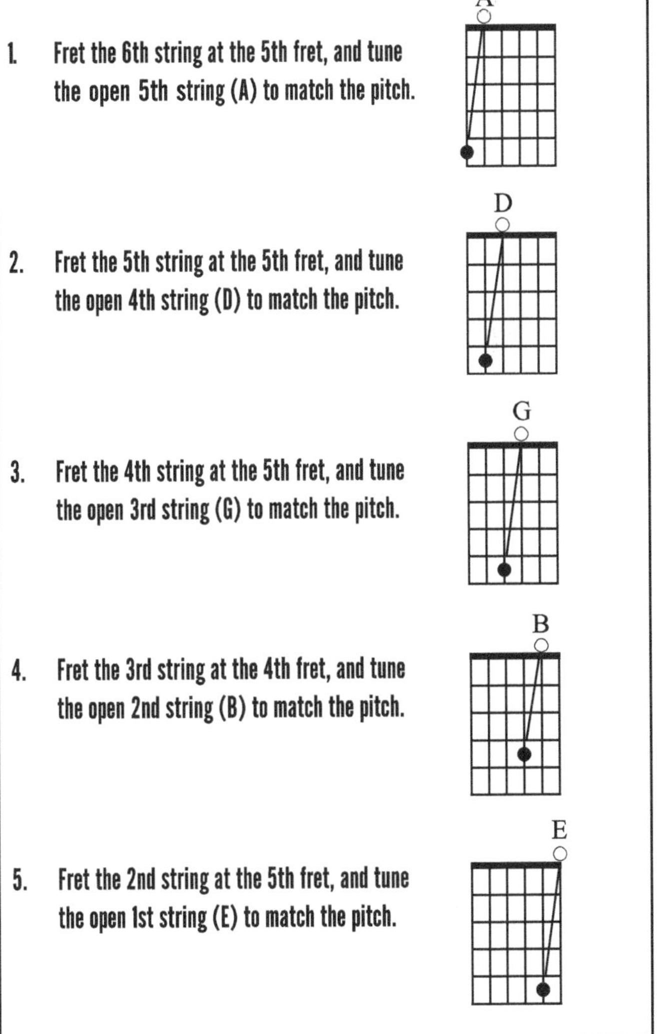

Tuning the guitar to itself.

MUSIC FUNDAMENTALS

Notes and Rests

In music notation, *notes* and *rests* are the basic symbols used to indicate rhythm. *Rhythm* refers to the duration, length, or time value given to a note or rest. The *quarter note* and *quarter rest* generally represent the basic *beat* or *pulse* in music.

Quarter notes and rests receive 1 *count,* or *beat.* With your foot, tap the rhythm of each quarter note or rest with a *down-up* tapping pattern.

Count: 1 1
Tap:

Half notes and rests receive 2 beats. Tap the rhythm of each half note or rest with a *down-up-down-up* tapping pattern.

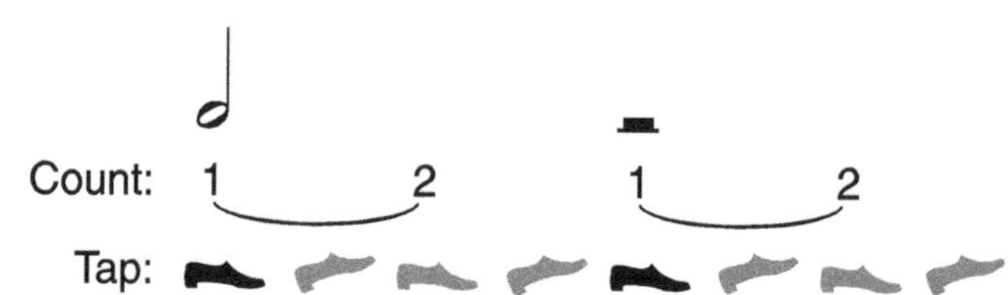

Whole notes and rests receive 4 beats. Use your foot to tap the rhythm of each whole note or rest with four *down-ups.*

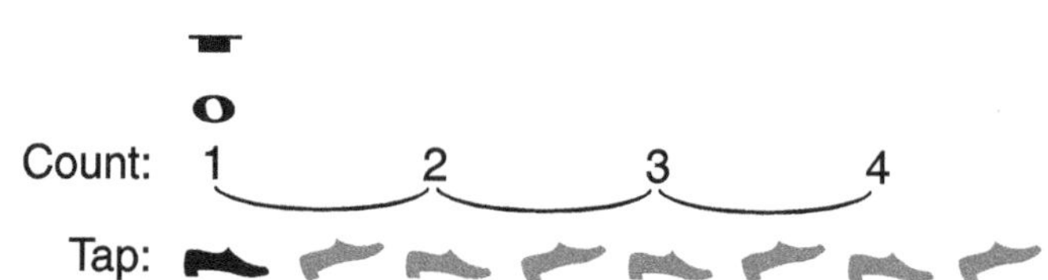

Slashes and Wavy Lines

A *slash* is an abbreviated way of indicating quarter, half, and whole notes. In guitar notation, it is used to show strum and rhythm patterns. A *wavy line* placed in front of a group of notes means to *strum* the strings.

Bar Lines, Measures, and Time Signatures

Bar lines are used to organize notes into *measures* that have the same number of beats in them. The most common placement of bar lines is every four beats. A *double bar line* is used at the end of a song. The most common *time signature* is $\frac{4}{4}$. The top number of a time signature indicates how many beats are in each measure; the bottom number tells you what kind of a note receives one beat. The time signature is placed at the beginning of the music.

Time Signature

4 = Four beats in each measure
4 = A quarter note receives one beat

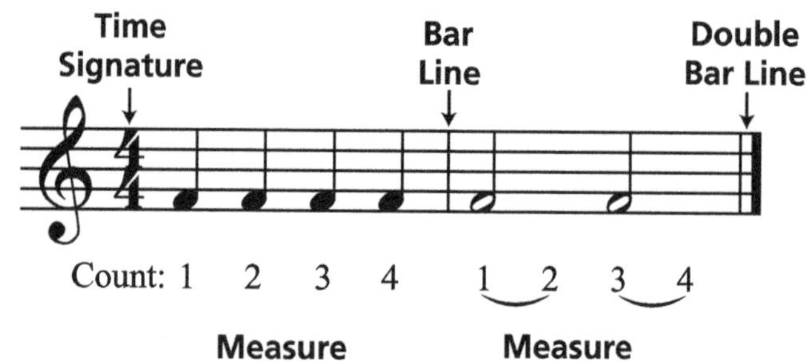

The Staff

Notes are placed on a *staff* to indicate their *pitch,* which is the sound's relative highness or lowness. The staff has five lines and four spaces. Notes can be placed on a line or in a space. The higher the note is placed on the staff, the higher the note sounds. In guitar notation, *numbers* placed next to the notes indicate fretting hand fingering, and *circled numbers* indicate the string of the guitar on which the note is located.

Staff

Lines

Spaces

The Clef Sign

A *clef sign* is added to the staff to indicate what the lines and spaces represent. Guitar notation uses a *treble clef,* also called a *G clef.*

The first seven letters of the alphabet are used to name to the notes: A, B, C, D, E, F, G. The names of the lines are E, G, B, D, F: **E**very **G**ood **B**oy **D**oes **F**ine. The names of the spaces are F, A C, E, which spells **FACE**.

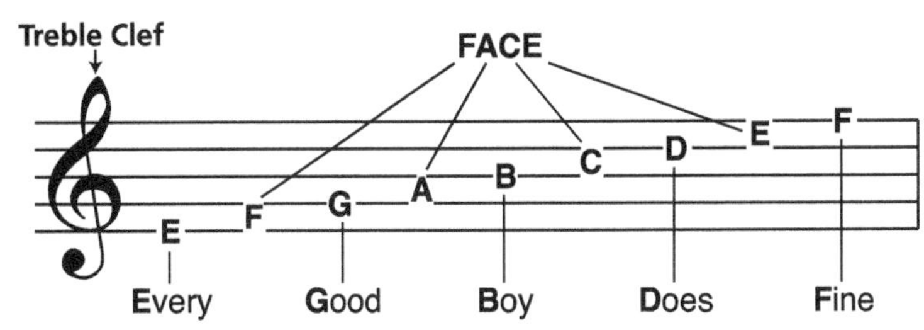

Chord Frames

Chord frames are used to indicate the placement of the *fretting hand* on the fingerboard. The chord frame represents the strings and frets of the guitar fingerboard, and numbers placed on the frame represent the fingers of the fretting hand. A zero stands for an open string, and an X means that string is not played.

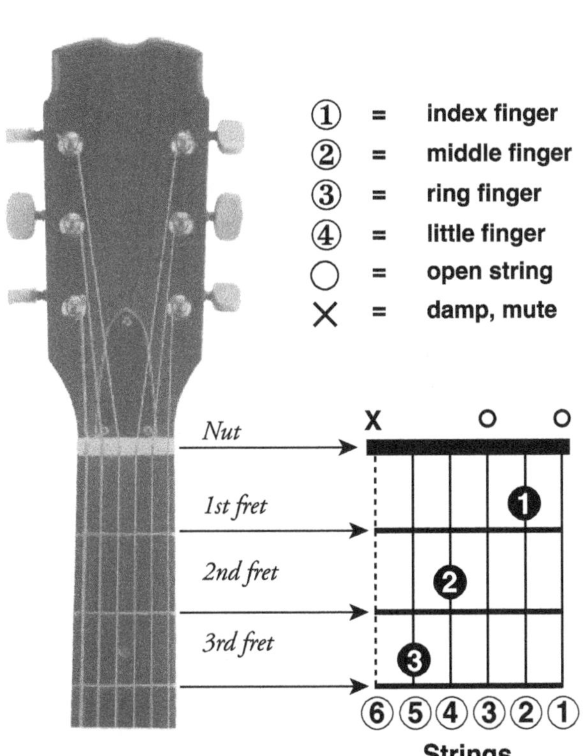

Tablature

Tablature (TAB) is a six-line staff that graphically represents the guitar fingerboard. A zero placed on a line indicates an open string, and numbers indicate the frets of the guitar.

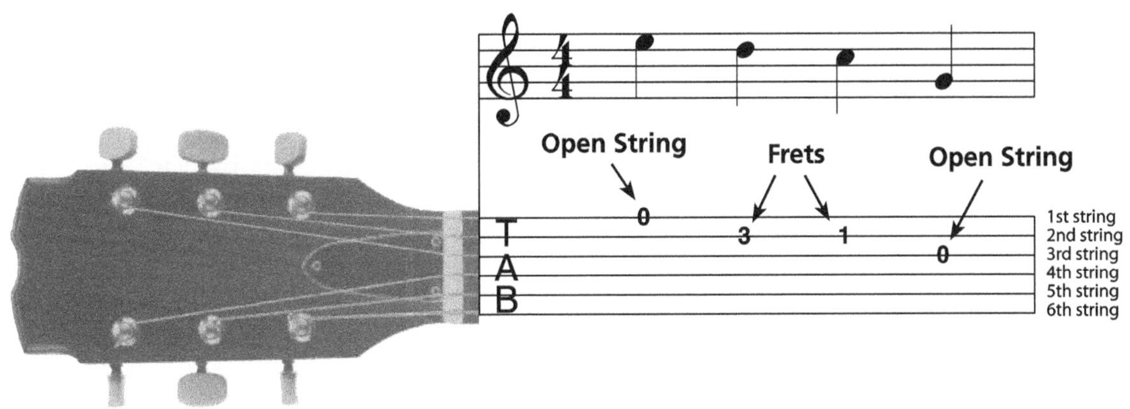

PLAYING POSITIONS

Playing positions vary somewhat, depending on the type of picking hand technique used, the type of guitar played, and the style of music performed. The following is a description of the basic fingerstyle and pickstyle playing positions for the guitar.

Sitting Position

Place the waist of the guitar on the right thigh. Tilt the guitar slightly towards you. Keep the neck of the guitar at an angle of 15 degrees to the floor. Rest the forearm on the edge of the guitar at a point just above the bridge. Bring the left hand up to the neck of the guitar. The wrist should be kept as straight as possible. When playing certain chords, you may need to arch the wrist slightly toward the floor.

Classical Position

Sit erect and forward in a chair. It is important to keep your back straight. Elevate the left foot by placing it on a footstool. The left knee should be slightly higher than the hip. Place the waist of the guitar on the left thigh. Tilt the guitar slightly toward you. You should be looking over the sound hole at the point where the fingerboard ends. Hold the neck of the guitar at an angle of approximately 35 degrees up from the floor. The head of the guitar will be approximately at ear level. Rest the forearm on the edge of the guitar at a point just above the bridge base.

You can eliminate the use of a footstool by using an A-frame (with suction cups) that attaches to the guitar, or a cushion designed to rest on the left leg to elevate the guitar.

Standing Position

When standing, use a strap to hold the guitar. Even in the standing position, the placement of the forearm should be on the edge of the guitar just above the bridge base. A strap for an acoustic guitar is attached to both the end pin and a strap pin on the bottom side of the guitar where the heel of the neck joins the body. Electric guitars have a strap button on the body of the guitar in addition to the end pin.

FRETTING HAND POSITION

The wrist of the fretting hand should be kept straight; however, there are some chords that will require you to slightly arch the wrist. The fingernails need to be short so that you can depress the strings. To achieve a good sound and to avoid "buzzing," you need to depress the string as close to the fret wire as possible. Buzzing occurs when the fretting finger is too far from the fret wire. The palm of the hand should not touch or cradle the neck of the guitar and the thumb needs to be placed on the back of the neck of the guitar so that it can oppose the fingers in a grip position. How far the thumb extends beyond the back of the guitar neck depends on the width of the neck and the size of the hand.

Finger position.

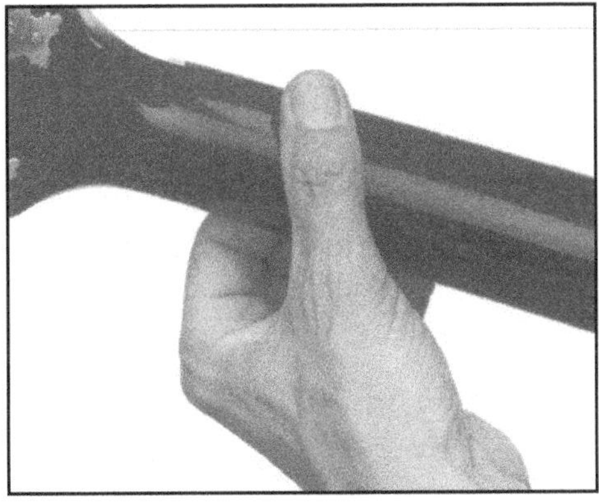

Thumb position.

Strumming Techniques

Fingerstyle

With the forearm resting on the edge of the guitar just above the bridge base, allow the picking hand to hang down in a natural manner. Keep the fingers approximately above the rosette and the thumb extended toward the sound hole. Keep the fingers slightly curved and bunched together.

Hand position.

Now *brush* (*strum*) down (low to high) across the strings with the index and middle fingers, using the fingernails to make contact. The motion of the strum is primarily from the fingers. If the fingers are properly curved, simply open up the hand and strum across the strings. You will achieve the best sound by strumming at a 90-degree angle to the strings.

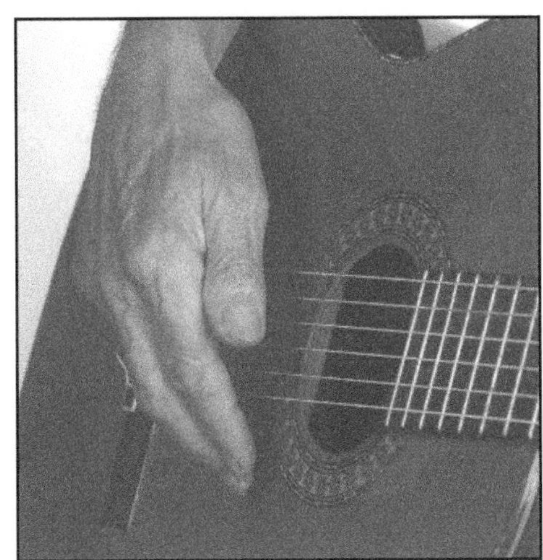

Brush strum.

Pickstyle

Use a *pick* (plectrum, flat-pick) to strum the strings. I recommend a medium gauge (thickness) *pear shape* or *drop shape* pick.

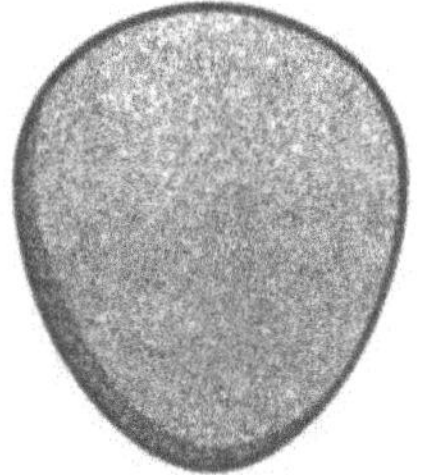

Pear shape.

Drop shape.

The pick should be held between the thumb and index finger. Keep the thumb rigid, similar to the way you would hold keys when opening a door. Place the forearm on the edge of the guitar above the bridge. Strum downward, perpendicular to the strings.

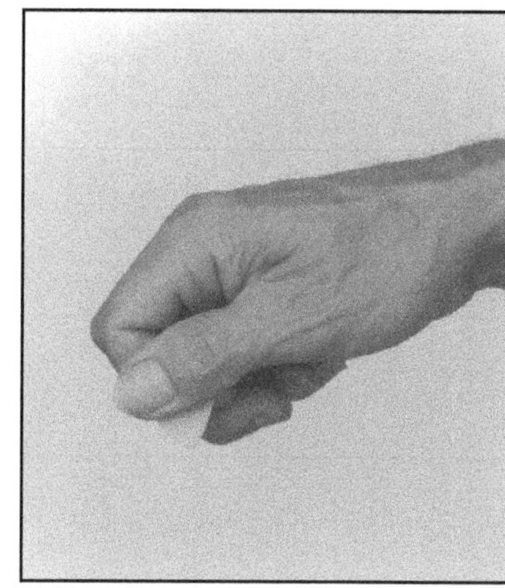

Holding the pick.

Arm position.

The angle of the pick to the strings should be fairly upright, at an angle of approximately 85 degrees toward the higher-pitched string.

Pick Angle

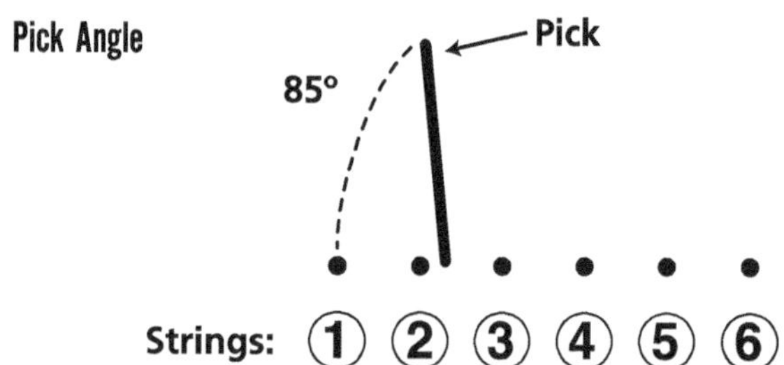

Beginning Strum

When you strum the strings of the guitar with the fingers or a pick, you will achieve the best sound if you strum perpendicular to the strings; that is, strum at a 90-degree angle to the strings.

Strum Technique

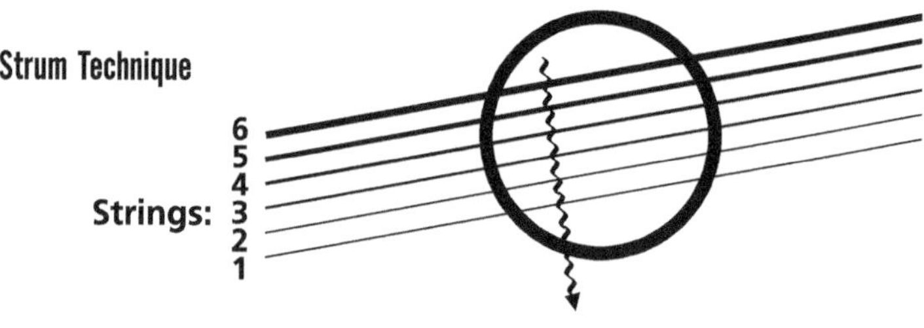

With the fingers or a pick, strum down across the open strings of the guitar to play example 1.

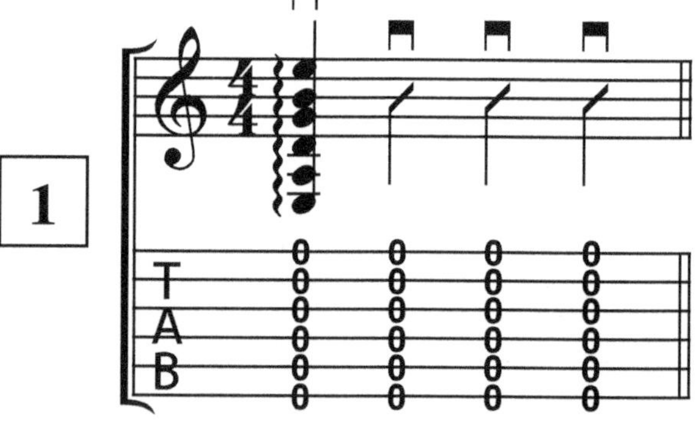

SECTION ONE: CHORDS & ACCOMPANIMENT

KEY OF D

D Chord

In the key of D, the D chord functions as "home base." Songs in the key of D almost always begin and end on the D chord. Place the fingers of the fretting hand just behind the frets. If the fretted string produces a "buzz," you either need to press more firmly or move the fingers closer toward the fret.

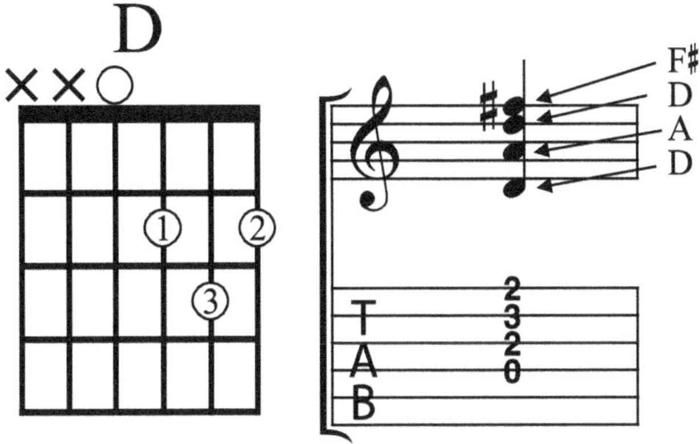

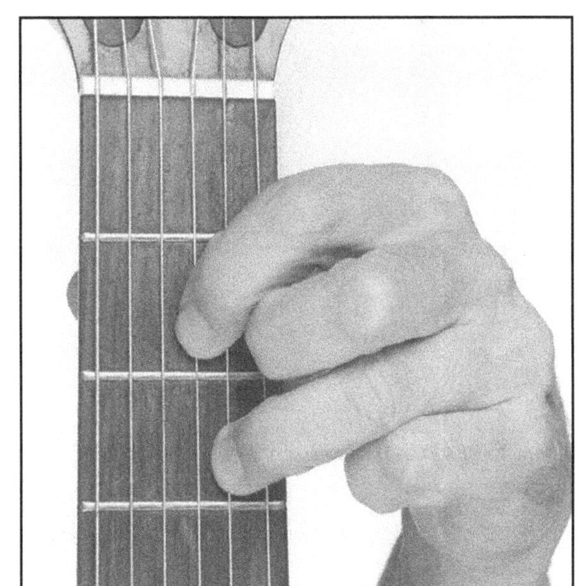

> ***THEORY***
> The D chord is built upon the first tone (*do*) of the D scale and is called the *tonic* or *I chord.*

A7 Chord

In the key of D, the A7 chord plays a dominant role. Notice that most of the songs in the key of D end with the chord progression A7 to D. The A7 chord contains a C-sharp (C♯).

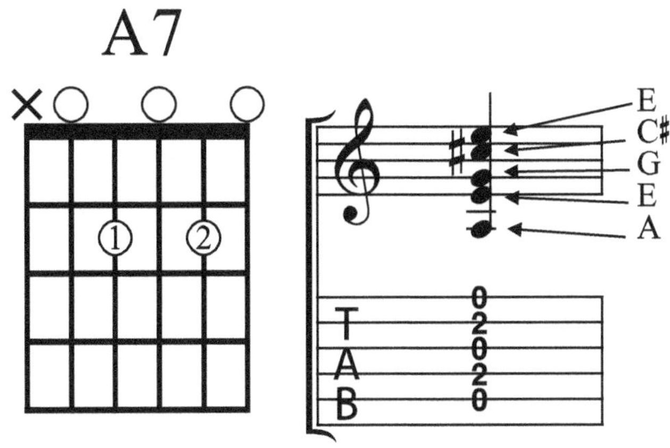

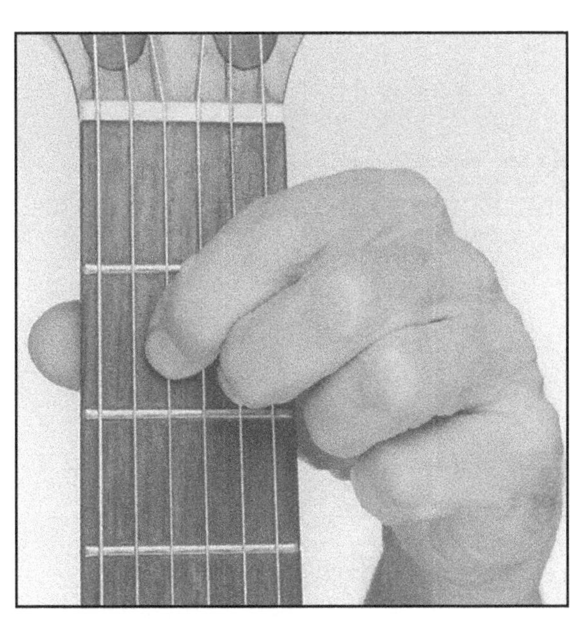

> ***THEORY***
> The A7 chord is built on the fifth tone (*sol*) of the D scale, and is called the *dominant 7th* or *V7 chord.*

Using a **down-stroke** with a pick or a **brush strum** with the fingers, practice the following chord drills. Strum the D chord from the 4th string. Strum the A7 chord from the 5th string. Repeat each drill several times. Each slash (/) represents one count and one strum.

Key Signature

D

CD 2.1

2

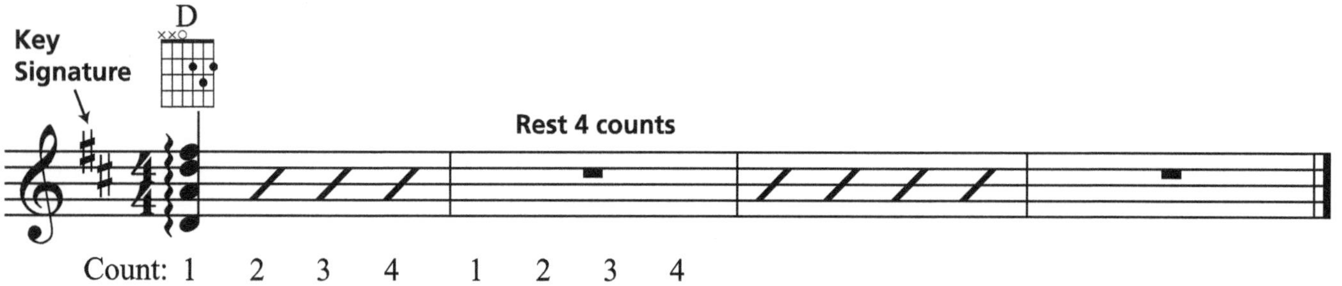

Rest 4 counts

Count: 1 2 3 4 1 2 3 4

A7

CD 2.2

3

D A7

CD 2.3

4

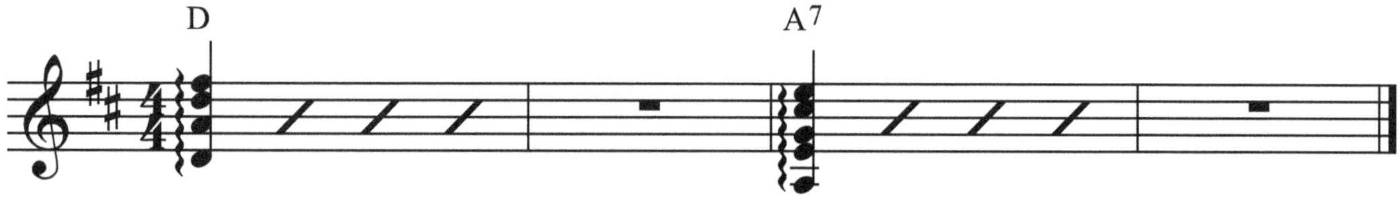

TRANSPORTATION: When changing from the D chord to the A7 chord, quickly lift the fingers of the left hand off the fingerboard simultaneously, and simultaneously place the fingers in the new chord position.

He's Got the Whole World in His Hands

PRACTICE TIP: *Slow is fast.* Practicing in "real time" is more beneficial than the "stop and start" method. Practice with a beat. A metronome is a valuable tool for practicing in real time. If it's too difficult to play at a moderate speed, slow it down enough so you can make the chord changes without hesitation. When you can play the chord changes at a slow tempo, play it faster, but never practice faster than you can handle.

Free Stroke (Thumb or Pick)

To execute a *free stroke* playing *fingerstyle*, pluck the 4th string with the thumb. Allow the thumb to continue moving forward and above the 3rd string. The thumb can come to rest on the side of the index finger (figs. 1 & 2). The motion of the free stroke comes from the joint where the thumb joins the hand; do not bend the thumb at the first joint. In guitar notation, the thumb is indicated with a lower-case, italic *p* ("pulgar"). This technique is also call *tirando*. For *pickstyle*, use a down-stroke with the pick, and stop short of the next string and immediately return to the starting position (fig. 3). The forearm needs to be on the edge of the guitar above the bridge base for both styles.

Fig. 1: Thumb preparation.

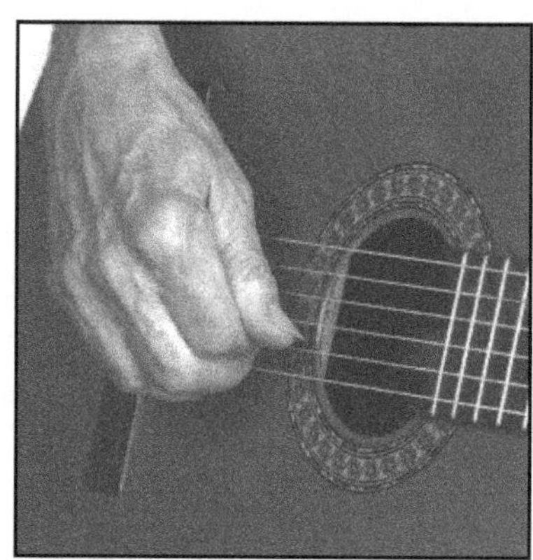

Fig. 2: Thumb completion.

Fig. 3: Pick preparation.

Primary Bass (Root)

Every chord is built upon a foundation or *root* (R), which gives the chord its name and functions as the *primary bass.* For example, a D chord has a D (open 4th string) as its root, and the A7 chord has an A (open 5th string) as its root. Play example 6 using down-stroke with a pick or free stroke with the thumb.

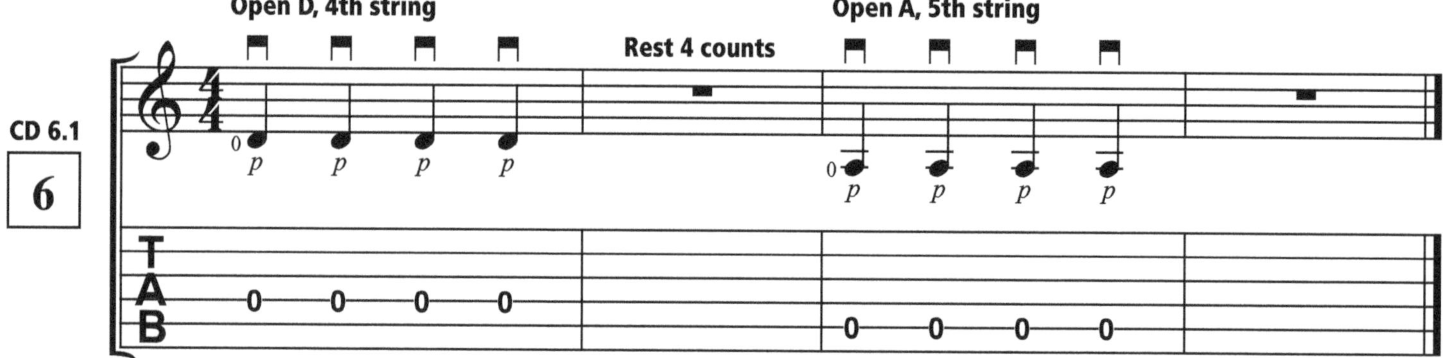

Bass Chord / Thumb Brush

When executing the *bass chord* or *thumb brush,* the root (R) of the chord is allowed to ring and followed by three downward strums across the top three treble strings (3rd, 2nd, 1st). Give emphasis (stress) to the root of the chord. In *pickstyle,* use a free stroke with the pick on the root, then strum downward across the treble strings. In *fingerstyle,* pluck the root of the chord with the thumb (free stroke) and brush the top strings with the index and middle fingers.

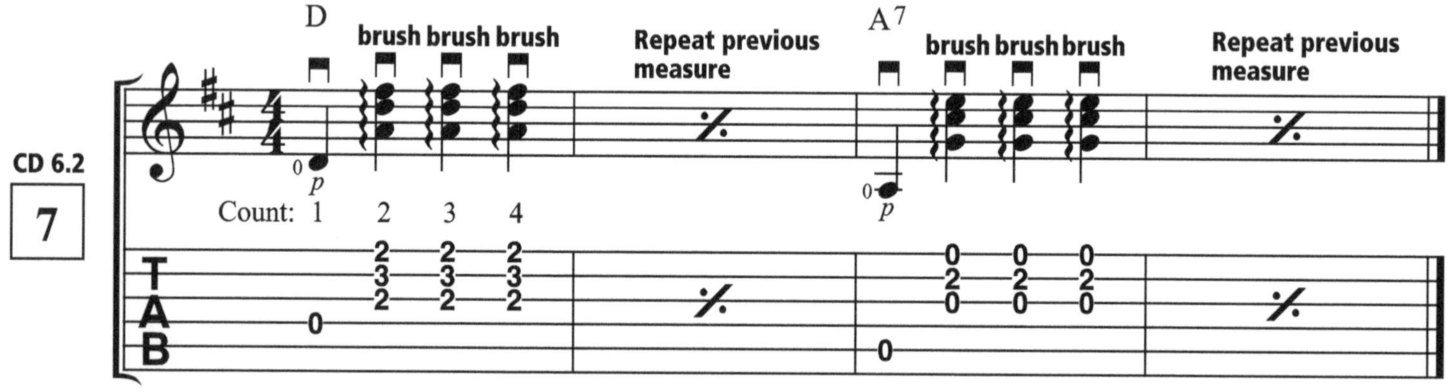

Puttin' On the Style

Traditional

CD 7 **Lively**

First Note

D A7

Put - tin' on the ag - o - ny, put - tin' on the style,

D

that's what all the young folks are do - ing all the while, and

A7

as I look a - round me, I'm ver - y apt to smile, to

D

see so man - y peo - ple put - tin' on the style.

Hey Lolly, Lolly Lo

Traditional

Bass Chord / Thumb Brush $\frac{3}{4}$

In *pickstyle*, use a down-stroke to pluck the primary bass note (the root of the chord) on the first beat of the measure, then, strum downward across the top three strings on beats 2 and 3. In *fingerstyle*, use the thumb to pluck the root of the chord, then use the fingers to brush down across the strings on beats 2 and 3.

Three-Quarter Time
8
D
A7
String: ④
Fret: 0
Count: 1 2 3
⑤
0

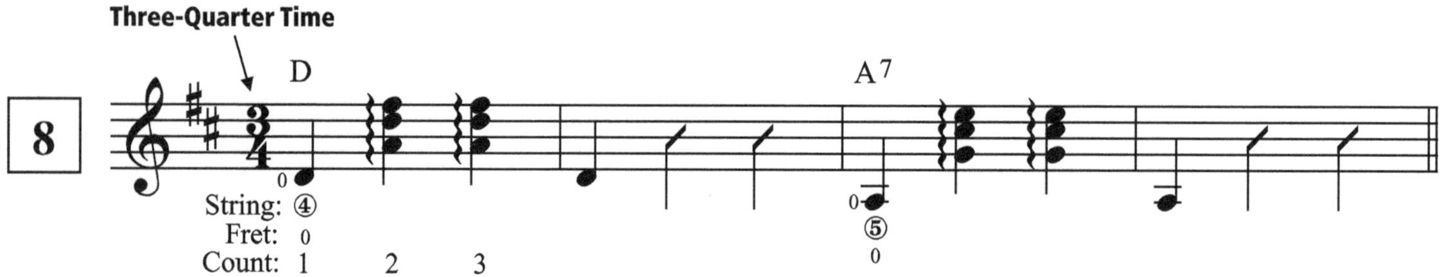

> ***THEORY***
> In three-quarter time $\frac{3}{4}$, there are three beats in each measure. The first beat should be emphasized, or stressed.

Down in the Valley

Traditional

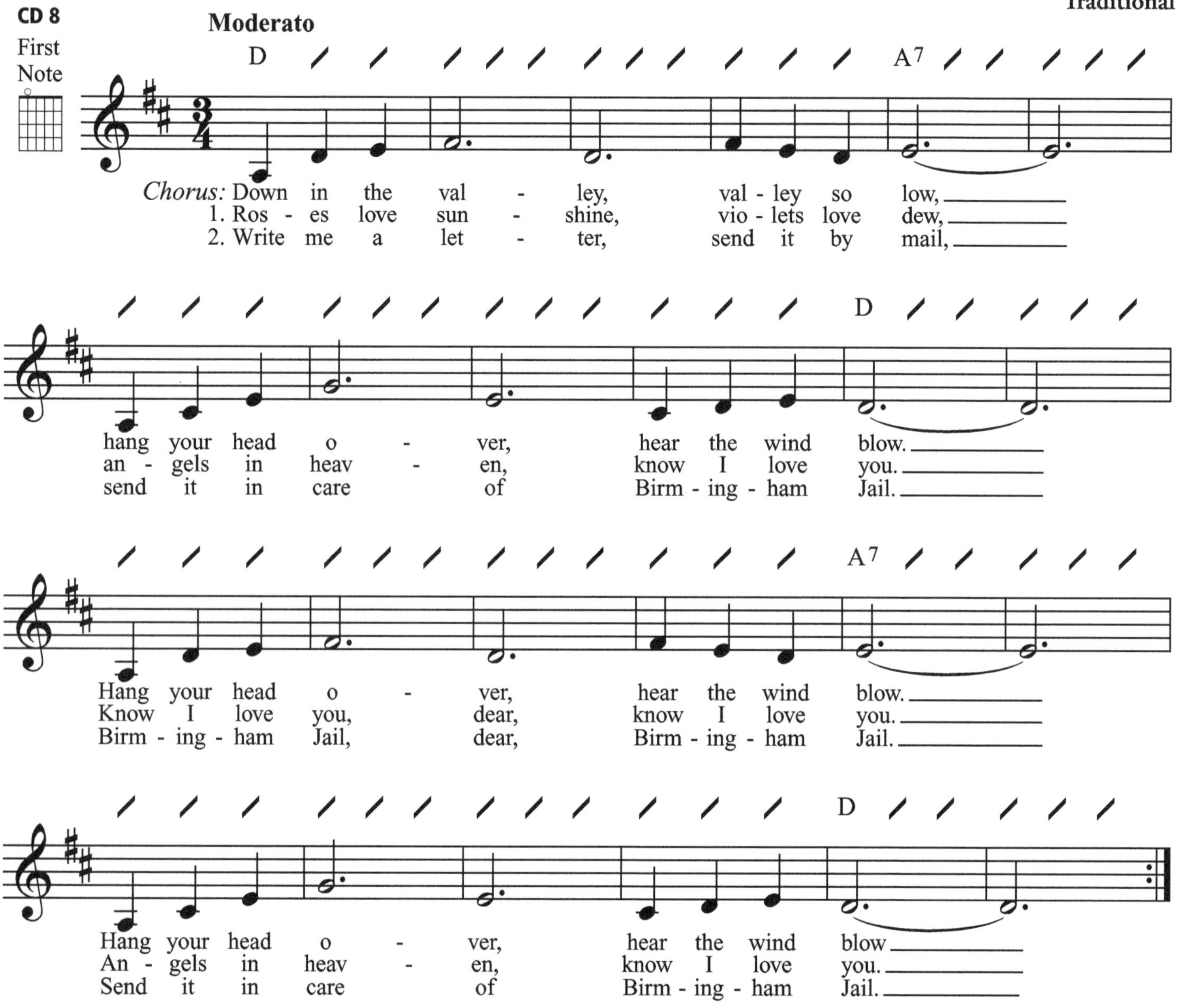

CD 8
First Note
Moderato
D
A7
Chorus: Down in the val - ley, val - ley so low,
1. Ros - es love sun - shine, vio - lets love dew,
2. Write me a let - ter, send it by mail,
hang your head o - ver, hear the wind blow.
an - gels in heav - en, know I love you.
send it in care of Birm - ing - ham Jail.
D
Hang your head o - ver, hear the wind blow.
Know I love you, dear, know I love you.
Birm - ing - ham Jail, dear, Birm - ing - ham Jail.
A7
Hang your head o - ver, hear the wind blow
An - gels in heav - en, know I love you.
Send it in care of Birm - ing - ham Jail.
D

G Chord

In the key of D, the G chord is the third most-frequently used chord.

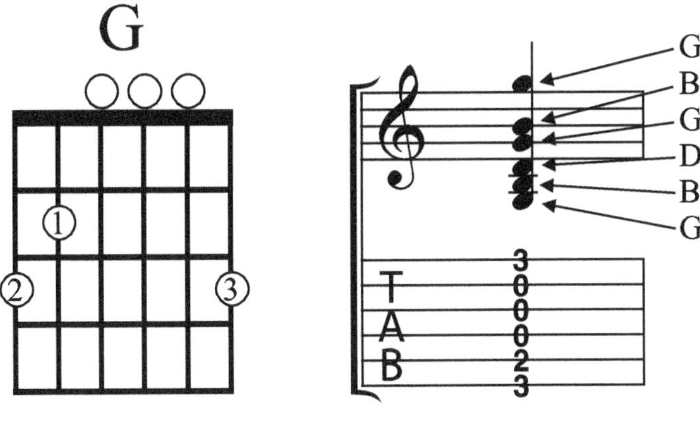

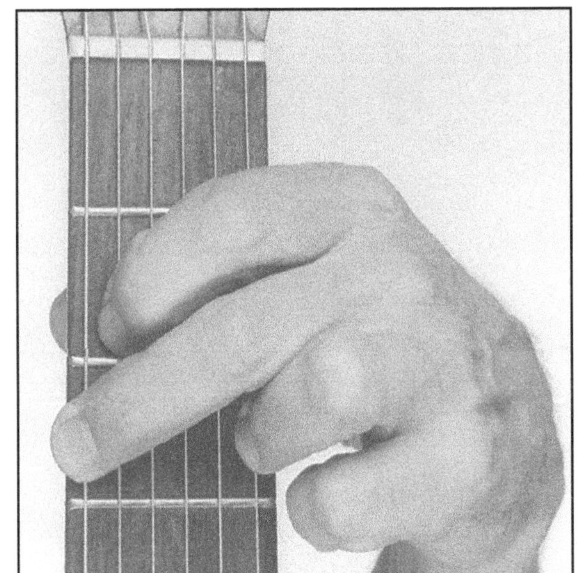

THEORY
The G chord is built upon the fourth tone (*fa*) of the D scale and is called the *sub-dominant* or *IV chord.*

You will be able to play the G chord without any difficultly if you closely observe the following:

1. A slight arc of the wrist of the fretting hand might assist you.
2. Do not allow the palm of the hand to touch the neck of the guitar.
3. The thumb makes contact with the guitar on the back of the neck, just past the middle of the neck.
4. The nails of the left hand must be short.
5. Depress the strings just behind the metal fret.
6. Strum the chord from the 6th string.

Optional Fingerings

If you have difficulty with the G chord, try the simplified versions in the first two diagrams shown below.

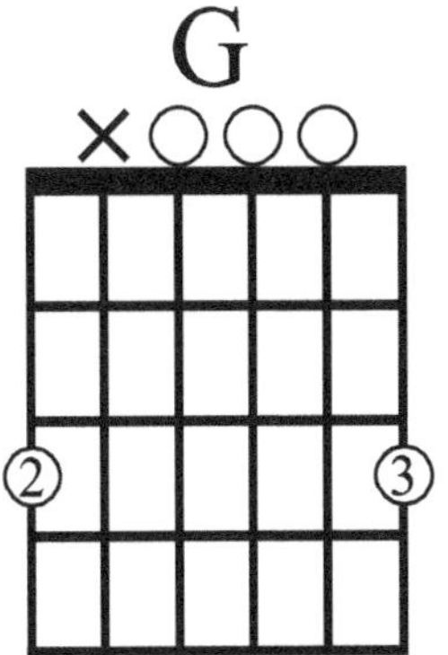

Allow the 2nd finger to touch (X) and deaden (silence) the 5th string.

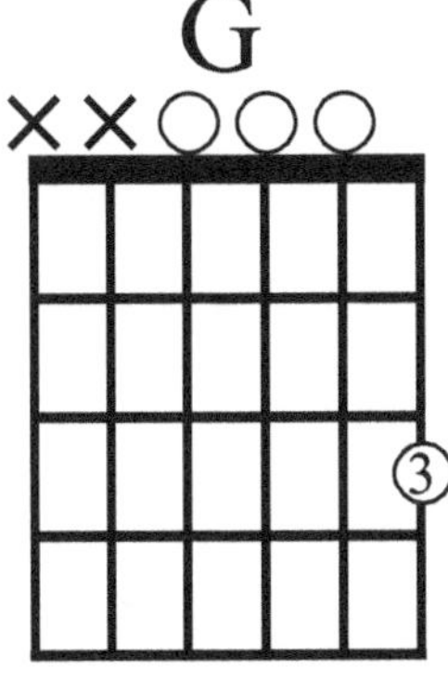

A simplified four-string version.

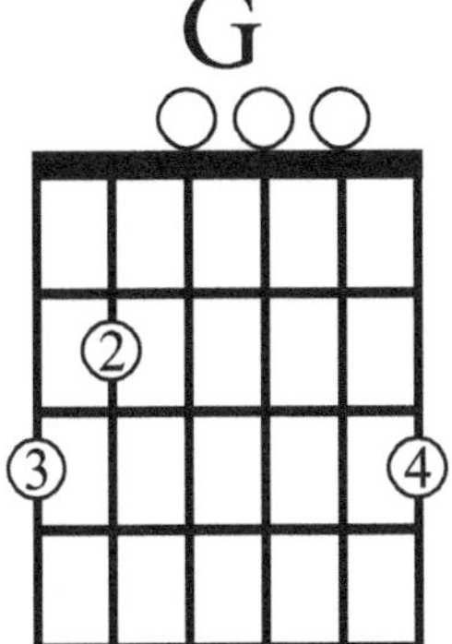

Most practical fingering when going to and from a C chord.

Play the following drills using down-strokes in *pickstyle* or brush strum in *fingerstyle*. Then, play "Beautiful Brown Eyes." Keep a steady beat.

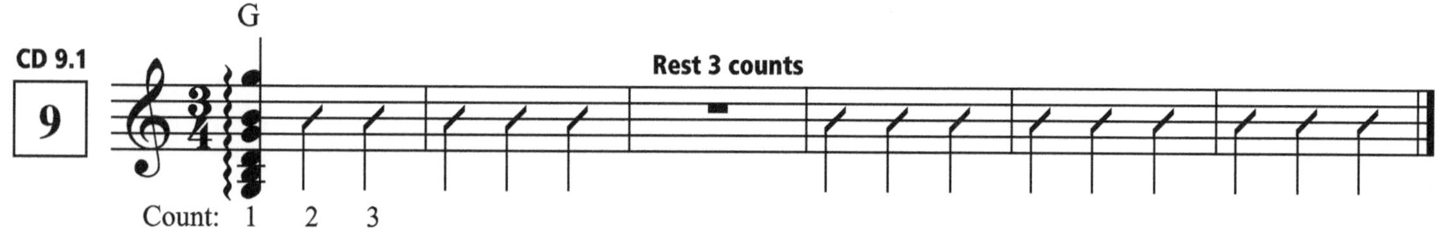

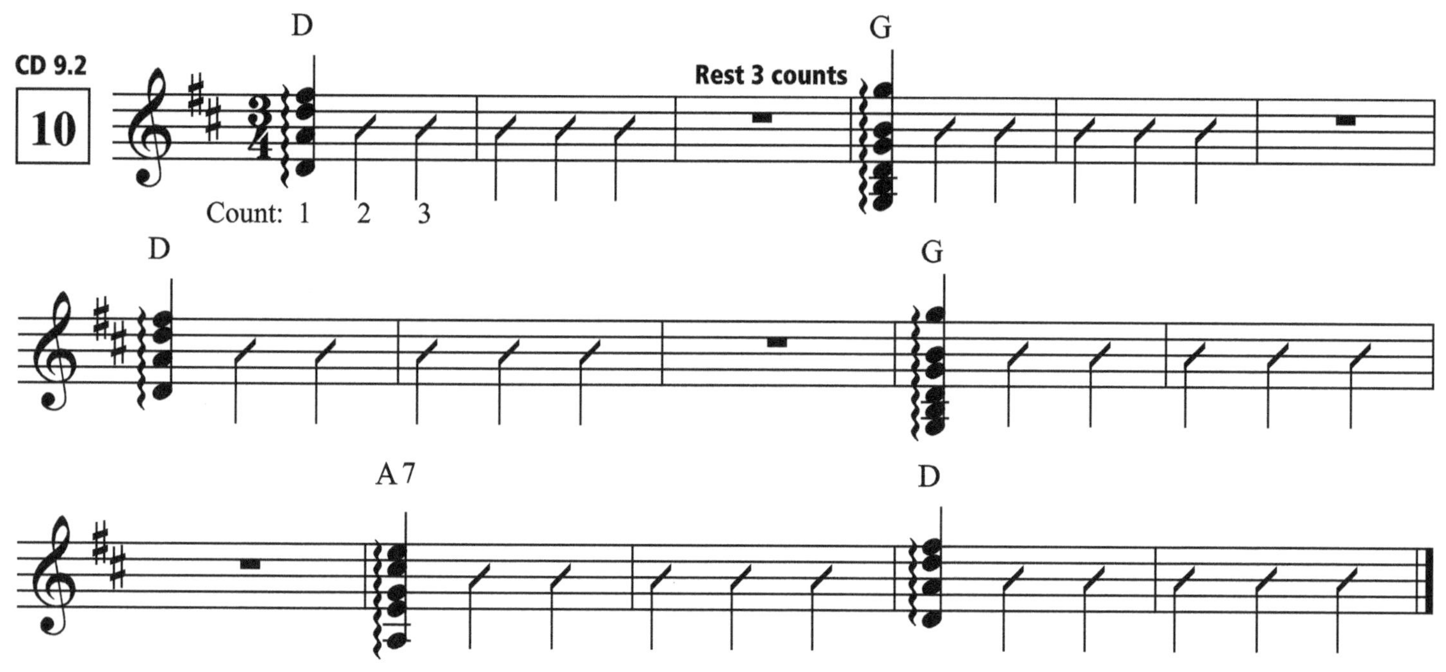

Beautiful Brown Eyes

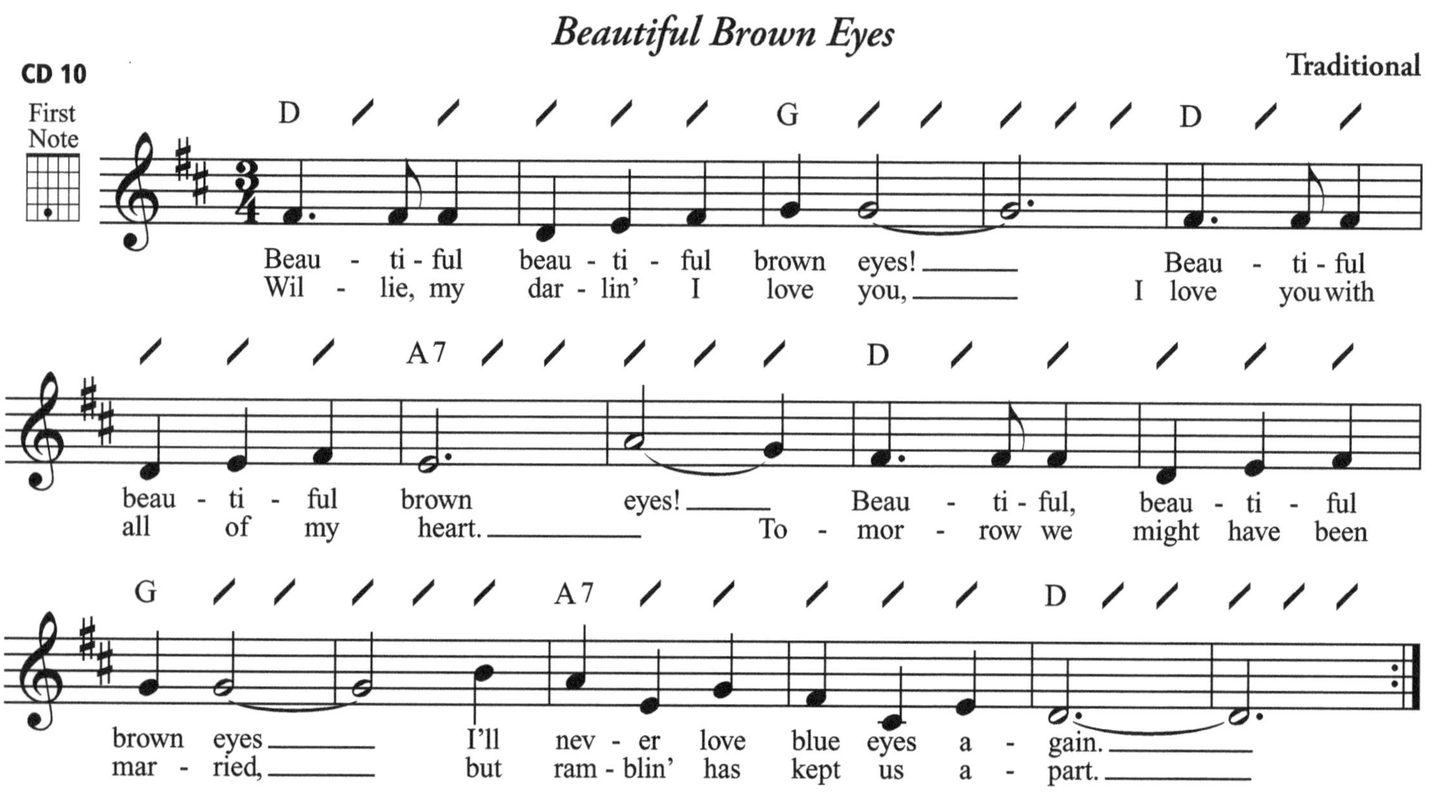

The root and primary bass note of the G chord is located on the 6th string, 3rd fret. Practice the following drill using free strokes with the thumb or pick. A dotted half note receives three beats, so hold each note for three beats.

11
String: ⑥
Fret: 3

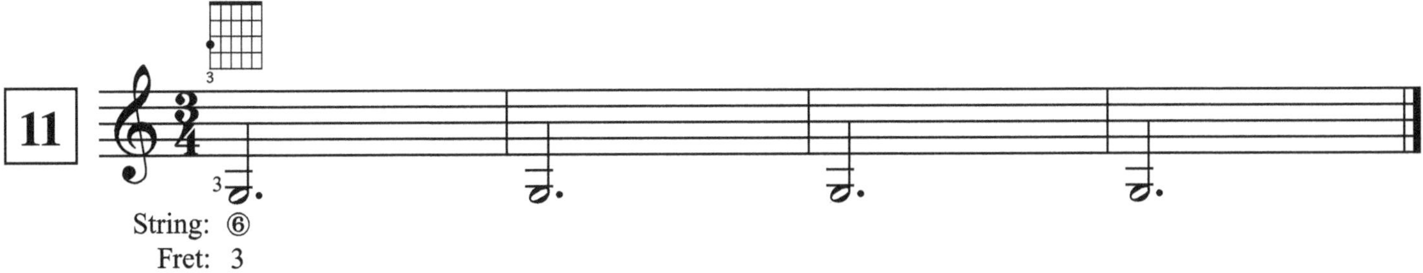

While holding the G chord with the fretting hand, in *pickstyle* play a **bass chord** pattern. In *fingerstyle*, play a **thumb brush** pattern strum. Pluck the root of the chord (let it ring), then strum the treble strings on beats 2 and 3.

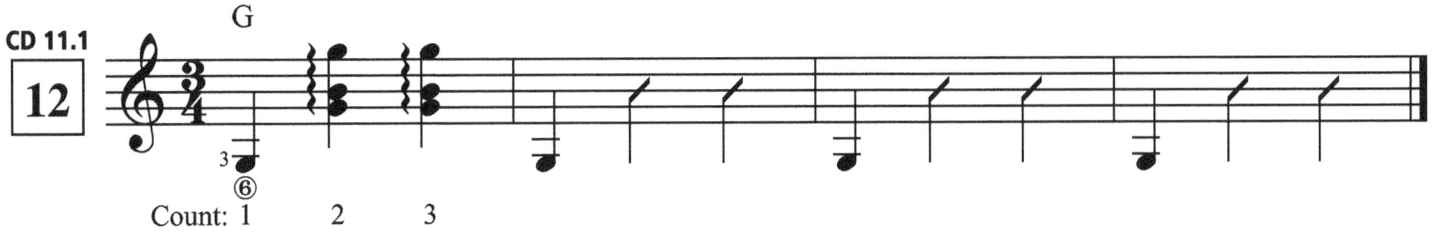

CD 11.1
12
G
Count: 1 2 3

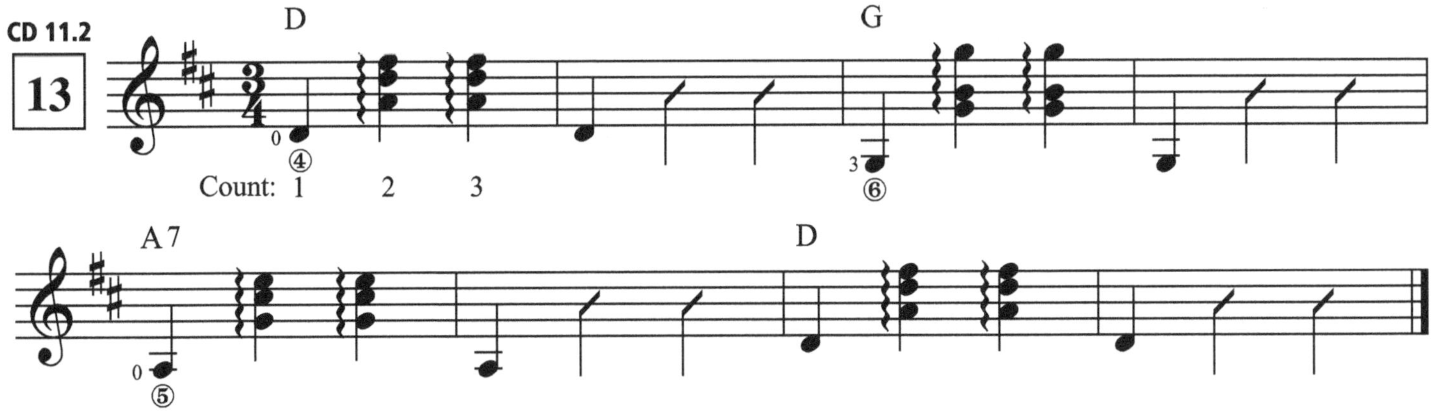

CD 11.2
13
D
G
Count: 1 2 3
A7
D

On Top of Old Smoky

Traditional

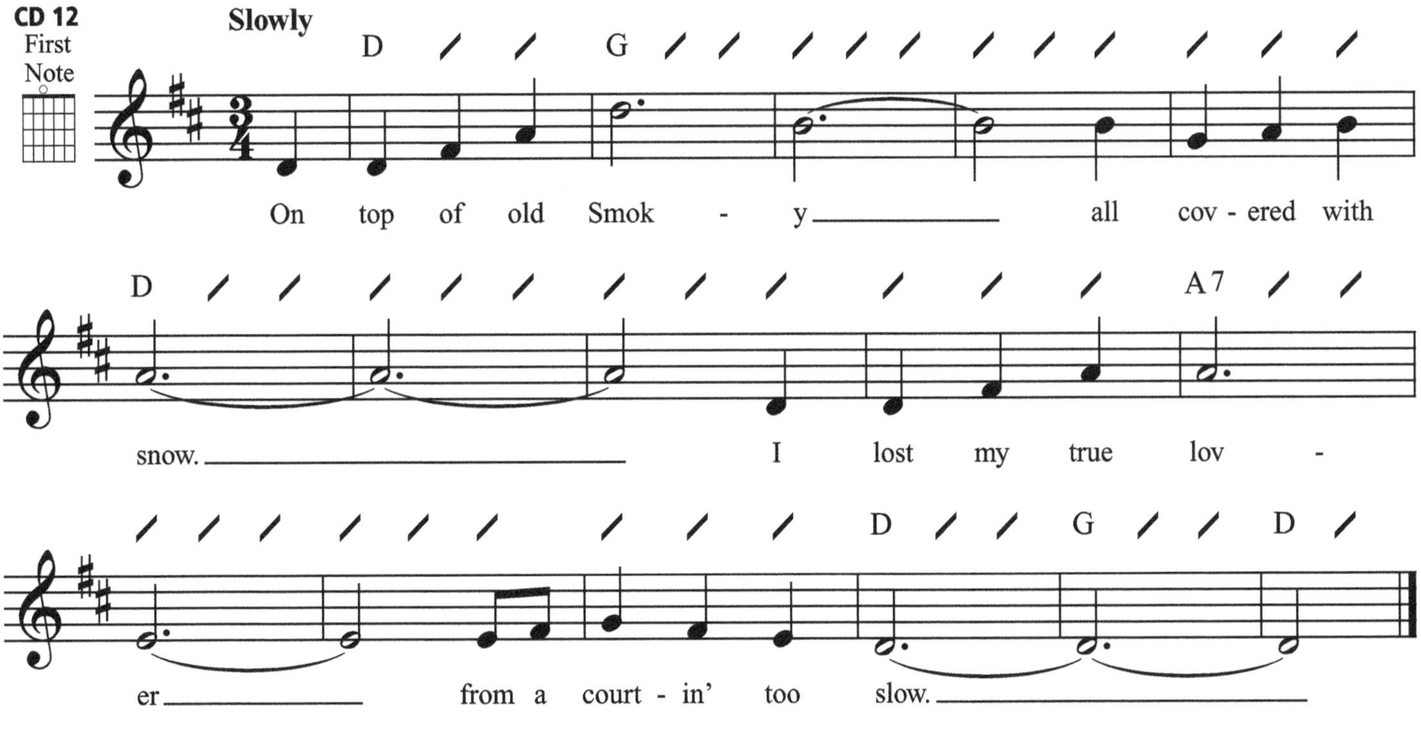

CD 12
First Note
Slowly
D G
On top of old Smok - y all cov - ered with
D A7
snow. I lost my true lov -
D G D
er from a court - in' too slow.

Bass Chord / Thumb Brush Alternating

Alternate the bass and the strum. Pluck the root of the chord on the first and third beats of the measure. Strum the top three treble strings of the chord on beats 2 and 4. Use either *pickstyle* or *fingerstyle* techniques. The strum should be performed with a minimum amount of movement in the right hand and arm.

Banks of the Ohio

Traditional

KEY OF G

Songs played in the key of G have their melody and chords based on the G scale. The G chord now functions as "home base," meaning the G chord is the *tonic* or *I chord.*

THEORY
The primary chords in the key of G are G, C, and D7. They are built on the first, fourth, and fifth tones of the scale.

G Scale and Primary Chords

D7 Chord

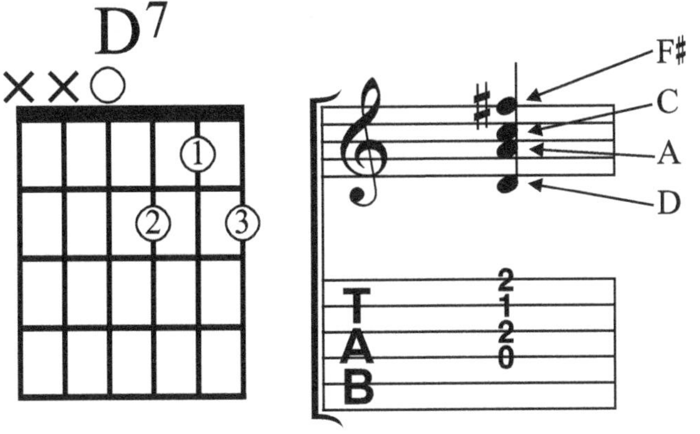

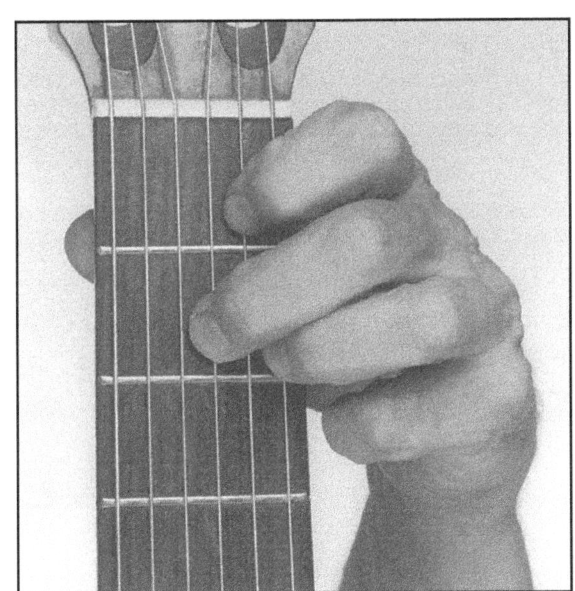

THEORY
The D7 chord is built on the fifth tone (*sol*) of the G scale and is called the *dominant 7th* or *V7 chord.*

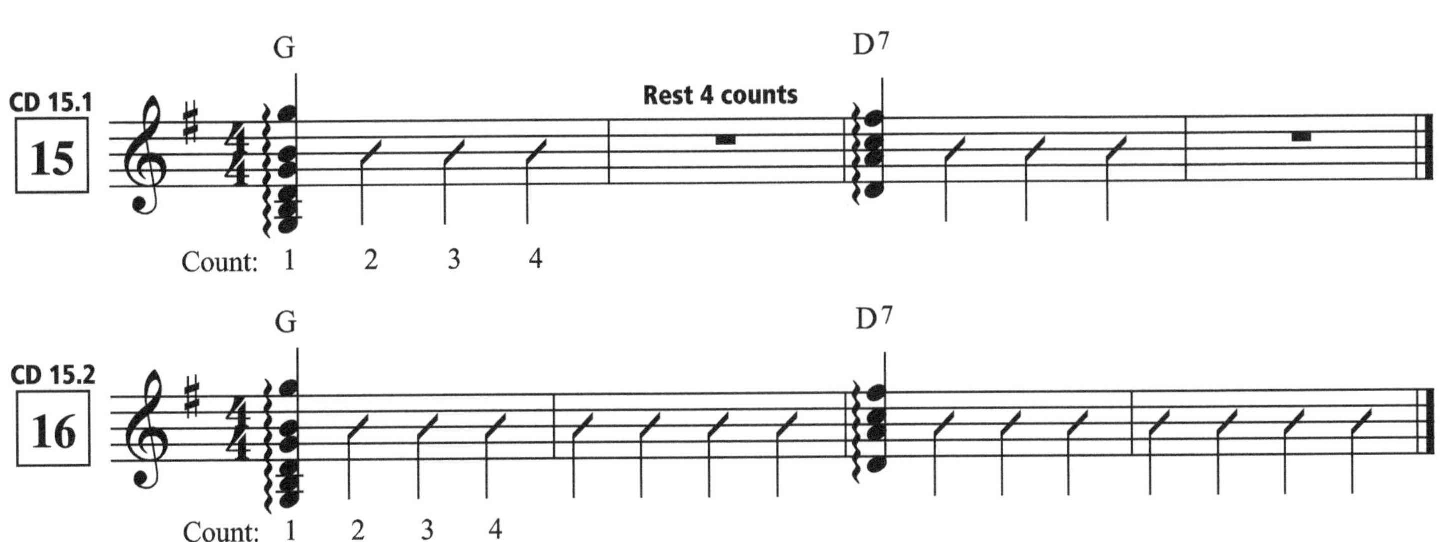

TRANSPORTATION
When changing from the G chord to the D7, or D7 to G, *slide* the 3rd finger of the fretting hand on the 1st string. Do not lift the 3rd finger from the string.

Tom Dooley

Traditional

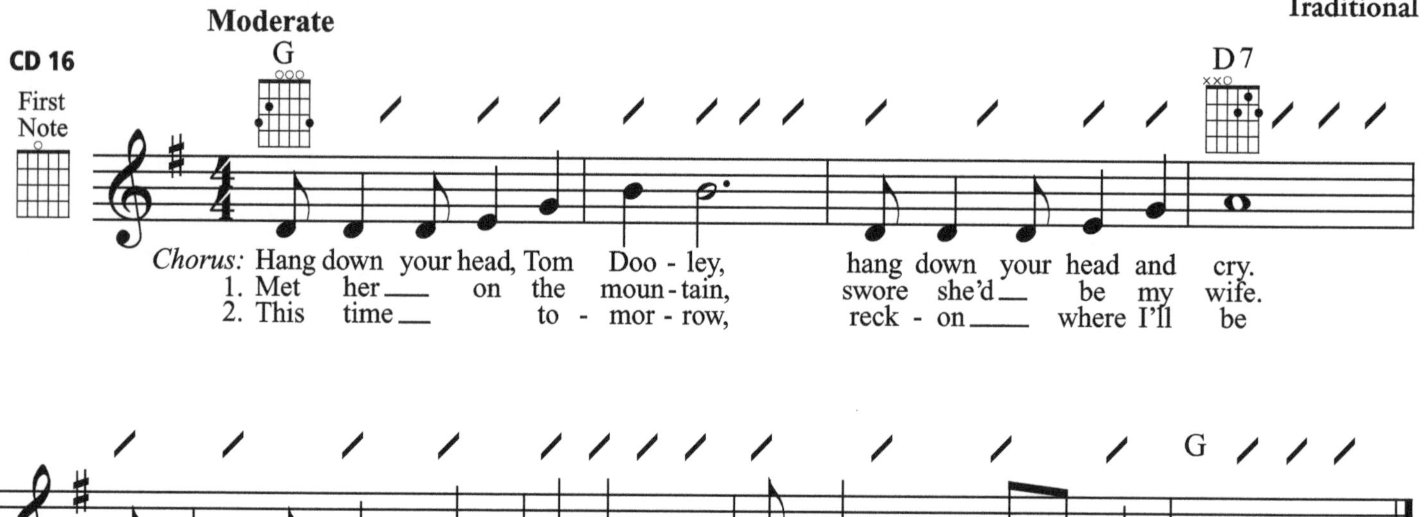

All the songs you have played in the key of D may be played in the key of G. "Good News" played in the key of G will sound higher. Changing a song to a new key is called *transposing*.

Good News

Spiritual

> **THEORY**
>
> Transpose "Some Folks Do" and "He's Got the Whole World In His Hands" to the key of G. Substitute the G and D7 chords for the D and A7 chords.

Bass Chord / Thumb Scratch Down and Up

In *pickstyle*, stroke the root (R) of the chord, then strum down (⊓) across the 3rd, 2nd, and 1st strings. Then, strum up (V) across the 1st and 2nd strings.

In *fingerstyle*, a *scratch* technique is used to strum the strings. The scratch is performed with the index finger and can be used as either a downward or as an upward strum. Pluck the root (R) of the chord with the thumb (*p*), then scratch down across the top three strings, and then scratch up with the fleshy part of the finger across the 1st and 2nd strings. The motion of the strum is from the finger. Do not move the hand out of its basic position above the strings.

> ***RHYTHM***
> Up to this point, all of the strums have been played on the downbeat. The downbeat is the regularly recurring pulsation in the music. Now divide the beat in half and strum or scratch up on the upbeat (&).

This Train Is Bound for Glory

Traditional

Moderate

CD 18
First Note

D

This train is bound for glo - ry this train.

A7

This train is bound for glo - ry this train.

D G

This train is bound for glo - ry don't ride noth - in' but the right-eous and ho - ly,

D A7 D

this train is bound for glo - ry this train.

C Chord

In the key of G, the C chord is the third most-frequently used chord.

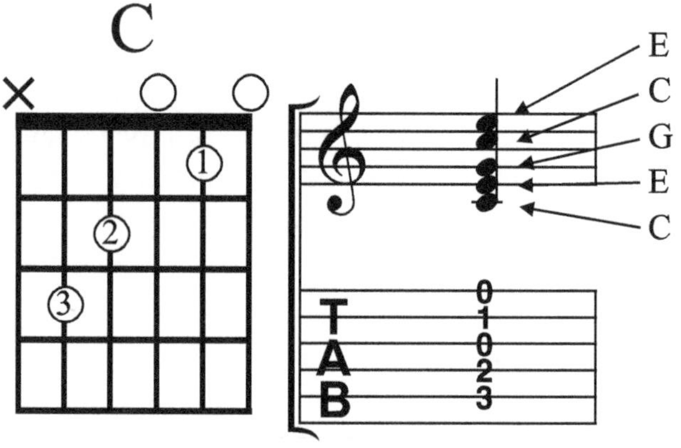

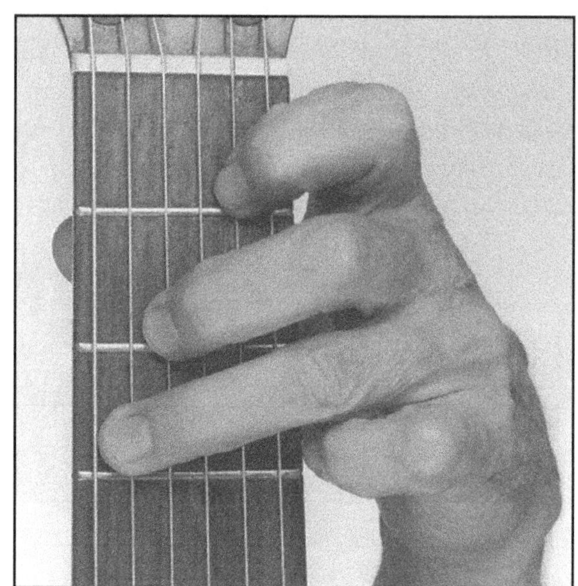

> ***THEORY***
> The C chord is built upon the fourth tone (*fa*) of the G scale and is called the *subdominant* or *IV chord.*

Using a down-stroke with a pick or a brush strum with the fingers, practice the following drill several times.

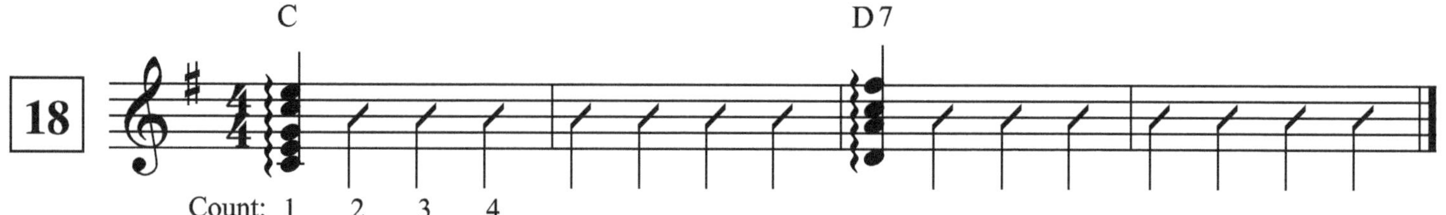

> ***TRANSPORTATION***
> When going from the C to the D7 or from the D7 to the C chord, keep the index finger of the fretting hand down.

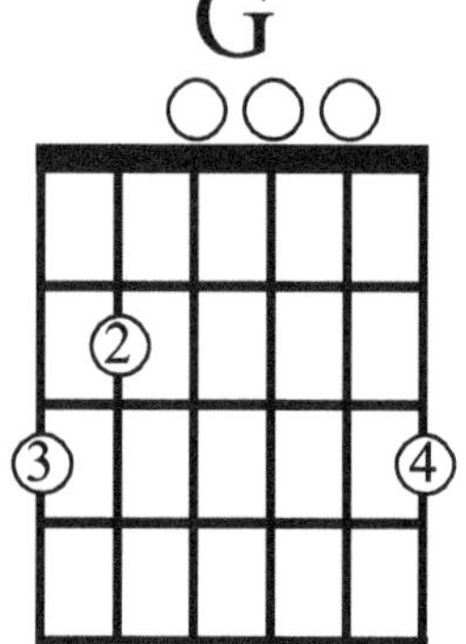

Although the weakness of the 4th finger will present a problem in the beginning, the following alternate fingering of the G chord is faster and easier when going to and from the C chord. Learn to use this fingering:

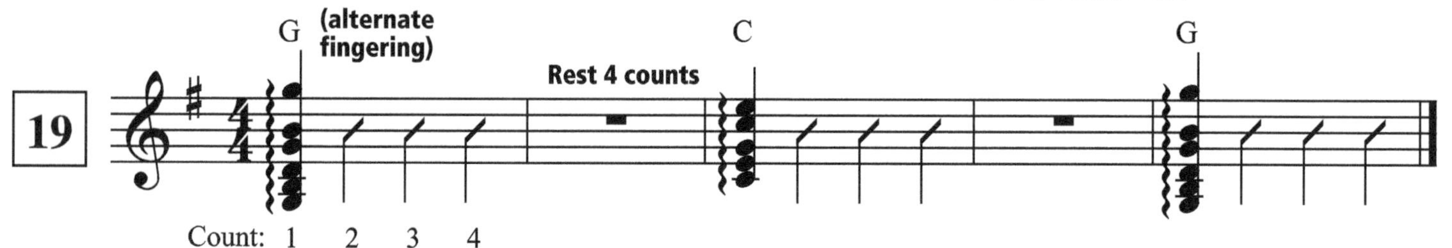

Worried Man Blues

Traditional

CD 19 **Moderately**

First Note

G

Chorus: It takes a wor - ried man to sing a wor - ried song. It
1. I went a-cross the riv - er and I lay down to sleep. I
2. I hung ___ down my head and cried just like be - fore. I

C G

takes a wor - ried man to sing a wor - ried song. It
went a - cross the riv - er and I lay down to sleep. I
hung ___ down my head and cried just like be - fore. I

takes a wor - ried man to sing a wor - ried song. I'm wor - ried
went a - cross the riv - er and I lay down to sleep, when I woke
hung ___ down my head and cried just like be - fore. I'm wor - ried

D7 G

now, but I won't be wor - ried long.
up, had shack - les on my feet.
now, but I won't be wor - ried long.

Give Me That Old Time Religion

Traditional

In the C chord, the root (primary bass note) is located on the 5th string, 3rd fret. Using a down-stroke with a pick or a free stroke with the thumb, play the following drill. Hold each note for four counts.

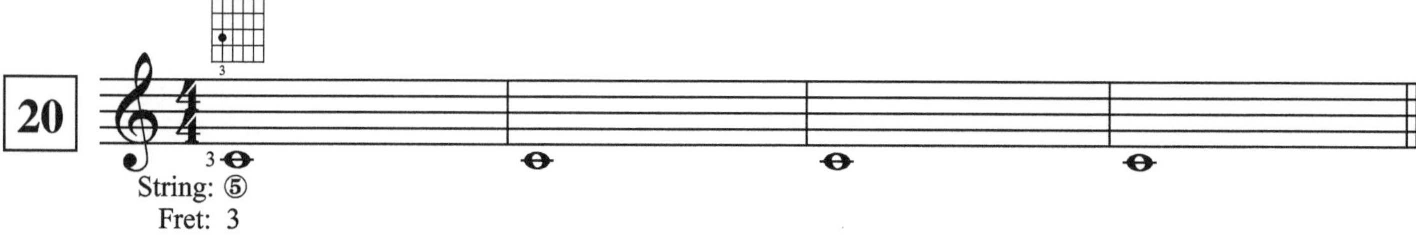

While holding the C chord with the fretting hand, pluck the root of the chord and then strum three times. Use either pickstyle or fingerstyle techniques.

After you are able to play the chord changes in "Study War No More," try using the bass chord or thumb brush strum. Pluck the root of the chord on the first beat of each measure. The root is located on the 6th string, 3rd fret for the G chord and on the open 4th string for the D7 chord.

Study War No More

Traditional

CD 20

First Note

Moderately

G

1. Gon-na lay down my sword and shield, down by the
2. Gon-na shake hands a - round the world, down by the

D7

riv - er - side, down by the riv - er - side,
riv - er - side, down by the riv - er - side,

G

down by the
down by the

riv - er - side. Gon-na lay down my sword and shield, down by the
riv - er - side. Gon-na shake hands a - round the world, down by the

D7

riv - er - side, down by the riv - er - side.
riv - er - side, down by the riv - er - side.

G

C G

Chorus: I ain't gon-na stud - y____ war no more, stud-y____ war no

D7 G

more. Stud - y____ war no more.________

C G

_ I ain't gon-na stud-y____ war no more, stud-y____ war no

D7 G

more. Ain't gon-na stud - y____ war no more.________

Bass Chord / Thumb Scratch Down and Up Alternating

While holding the chord with the fretting hand, **alternate** between the root and a down-up strum. The strum should be performed with a minimum amount of movement in the picking hand. In *pickstyle*, use a down-stroke on the root with an alternating down-up stroke on the chords. In *fingerstyle*, pluck the root with the thumb (free stroke) followed by a down-up scratch with the index finger.

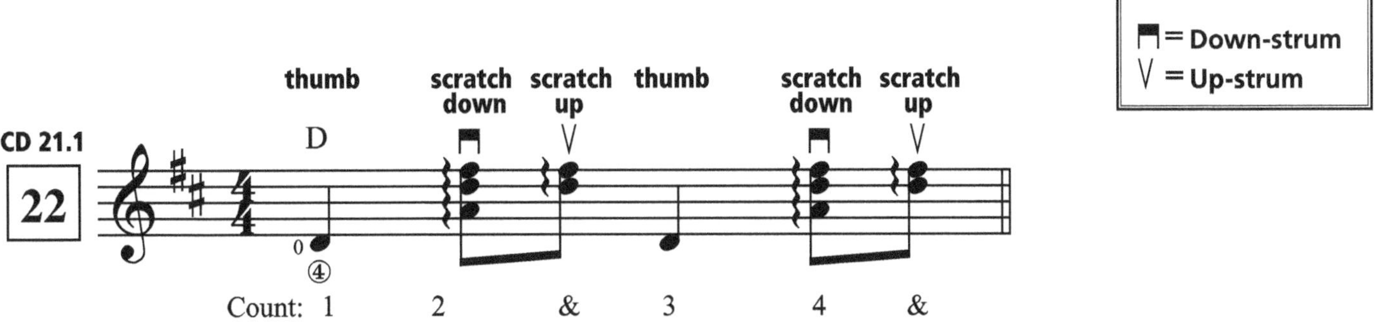

Now apply this strum to the G, C, and D7 chords. When you have the strum "grooved," apply it to "Study War No More." It is often helpful to practice strums on open strings so that you can concentrate on the picking hand technique.

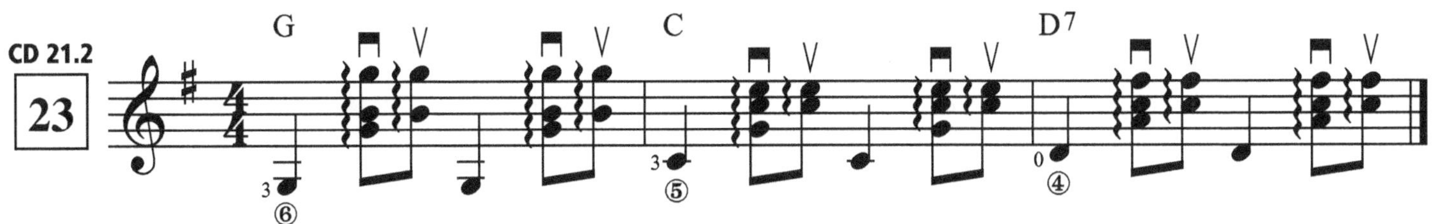

Alternate Bass (Fifth)

In all previous strums, you have plucked the *root* (R), the primary bass note, of the chord. It is possible to achieve a more interesting bass pattern by alternating between the root (R) and the *fifth* (5) of the chord. The fifth (5) is the most frequently used *alternate bass* note.

For the following exercises, pluck the root (R) on the first beat of the measure, strum the top three strings on the second beat, pluck the fifth (5) on the third beat, and strum the strings on the fourth beat. This pattern remains the same for all chords. Drill each of the following chords.

Memorize where the root and fifth are located in each chord. "Groove" the alternating bass strum pattern, and apply it to familiar songs. Review "Banks of the Ohio," "Tom Dooley," and "Worried Man Blues" using the alternating bass chord pattern.

After you have learned "The Midnight Special," try using the alternating bass chord strum pattern.

KEY OF A

Songs played or sung in the key of A have their melody and chords based on the A scale. The A chord now functions as "home base."

> **THEORY**
> The primary chords in the key of A are A, D, and E7. They are constructed on the first, fourth, and fifth tones of the A scale.

A Scale and Primary Chords

A Chord

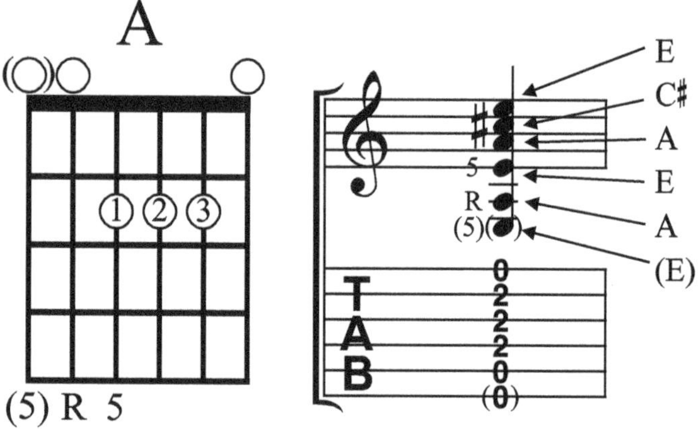

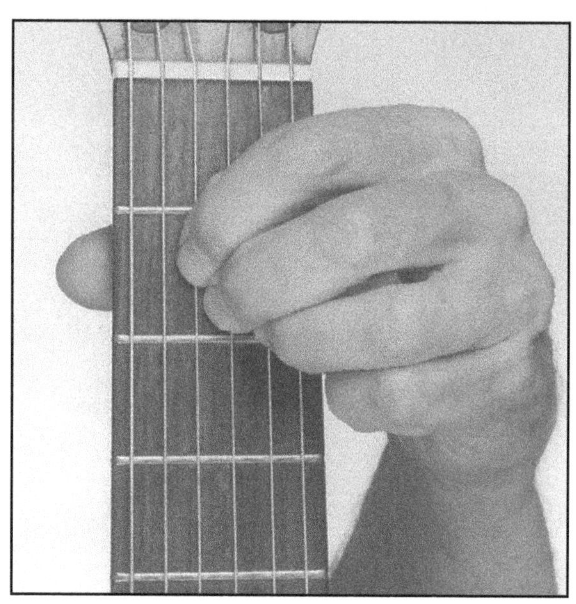

> **THEORY**
> The A chord is the *tonic* or *I chord* in the key of A. The primary bass (R) is located on the open 5th string. The alternate bass (5) is located on either the 4th or 6th string.

Optional Fingerings

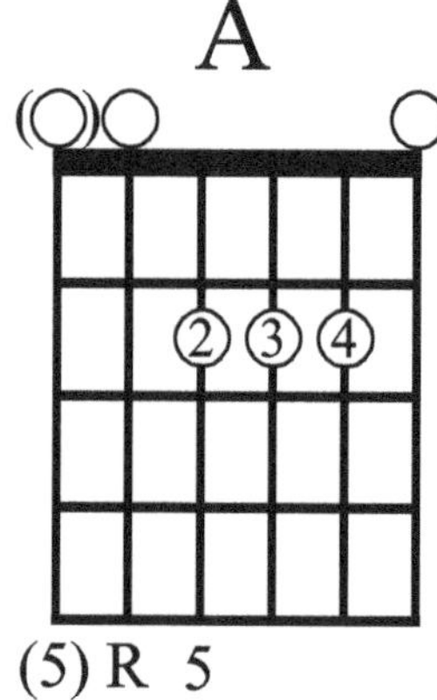

This fingering requires the least amount of left hand movement when going to the E7 chord.

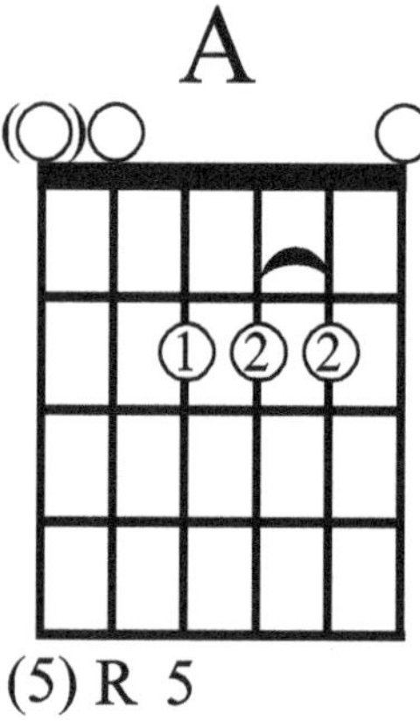

This fingering works best on guitars with narrow necks or for students with large fingers.

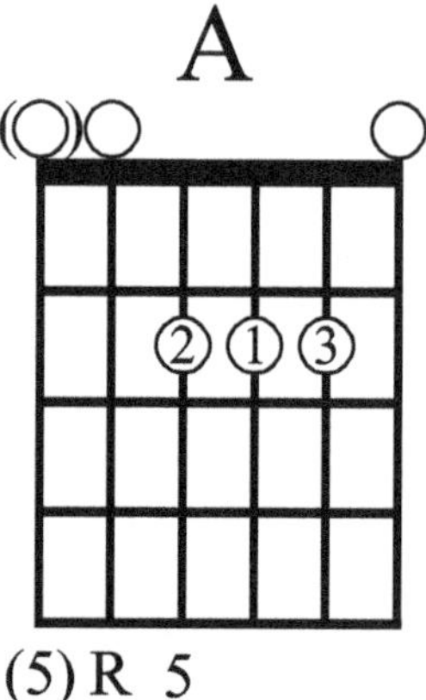

This fingering is similar in shape to the D7 fingering; not particularly recommended by the author.

E7 Chord

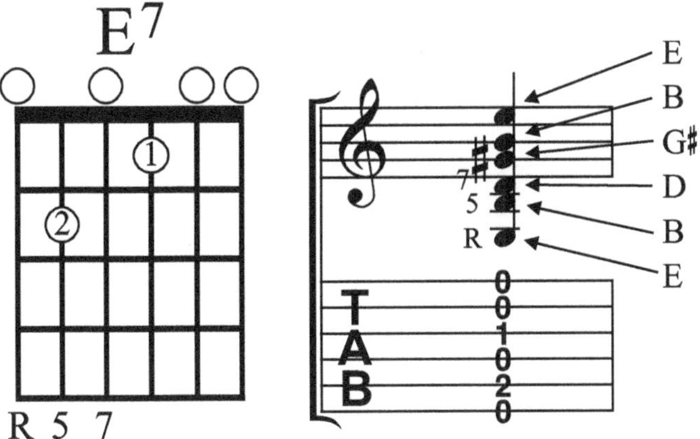

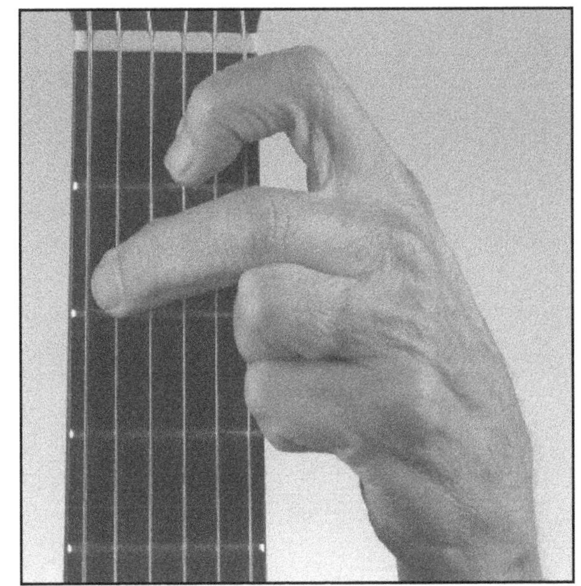

THEORY
The E7 chord is the *dominant 7th* or *V7 chord* in the key of A. The primary bass (R) is located on the open 6th string. The note on the 5th string, 2nd fret, is the alternate bass (5).

Optional Fingerings

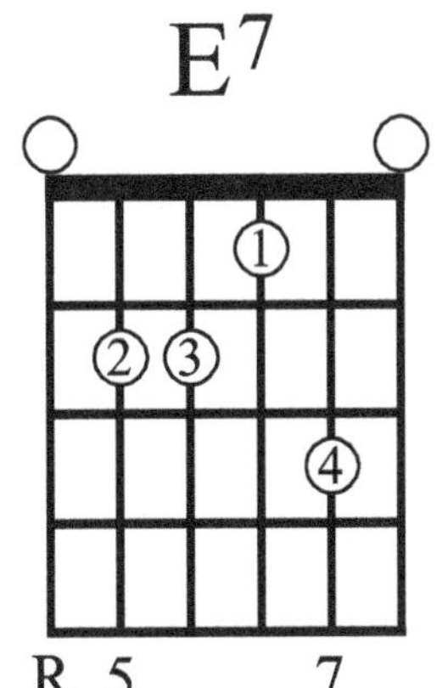

This form of the E7 sounds "richer."

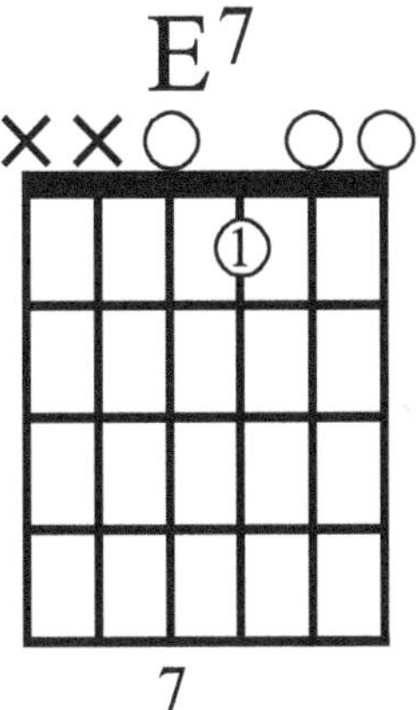

Simplified version of the E7 chord.

Using a down-stroke with a pick or a brush strum with the fingers, practice the following drills until you can make the change from the A to the E7 smoothly and without hesitation. Strum from the root (R) of the A and E7 chords. Try using different fingerings. If you have control over the 4th finger of the fretting hand, I recommend using the first optional A chord fingering on the previous page and the first optional E7 chord fingering above.

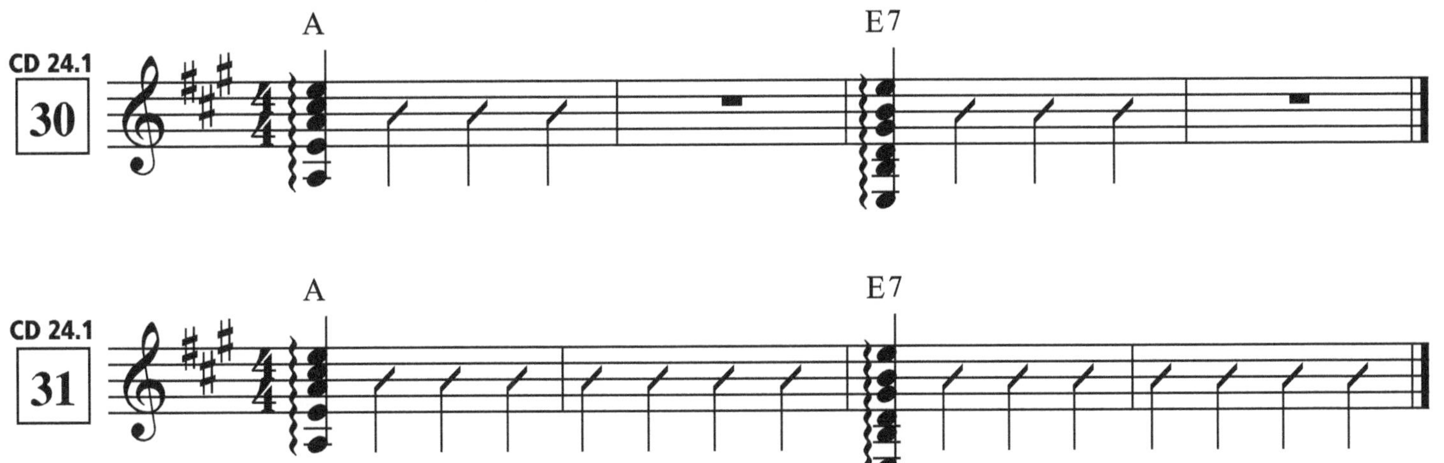

Just a Closer Walk with Thee

Sacred

CD 25
First Note

Slowly

A / / / / / / / / E7 / / / / / / / /

1. Just a clos - er walk with Thee,
2. I am weak and Thou art strong,
3. Thru this world of toil and snares,

/ / / / / / / / A / / / / / / / /

grant it Je - sus if you please.
Je - sus keep me from all wrong.
if I fal - ter, Lord who cares.

A7 / / / / / / / / D / / / / / / / /

Dai - ly walk - in' close to Thee. Let it
I'll be sat - is - fied as long as I
Who with me my bur - den shares? None but

A / / / E7 / / / A / / / / / / / /

be, dear Lord, let it be.
walk, let me walk, close to you.
Thee, my dear Lord, none but Thee.

Transpose "Give Me That Old Time Religion" and "Tom Dooley" into the key of A.

Alternate Bass (Fifth)

In the case of the A chord, when performing the alternate bass pattern, the fifth (5) may be played on either the 4th or 6th string. When playing the E7 chord, alternate between the 6th string (R) and the 5th string (5).

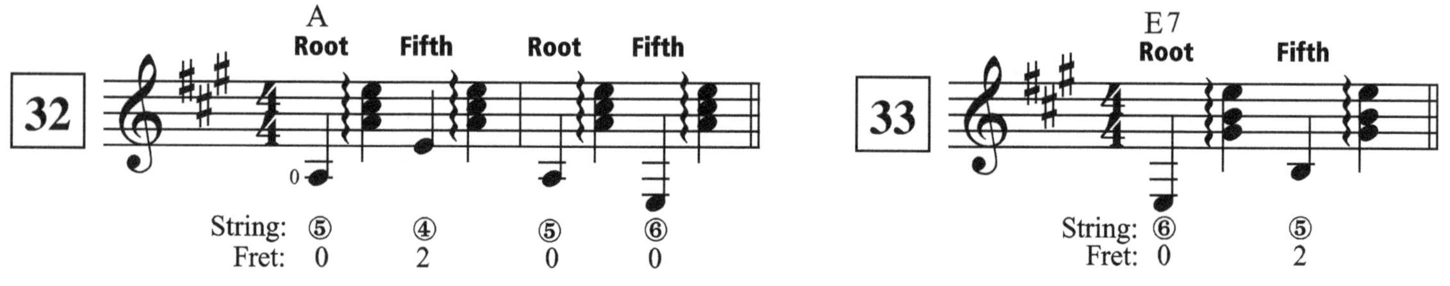

Swing Eighths (Shuffle Beat)

Eighth notes are played evenly, with each note receiving half of the beat. One note is played on the downbeat, and the second note is played on the upbeat. In most rock, Latin, and popular music, eighth notes played in this manner are referred to as *straight eighths.*

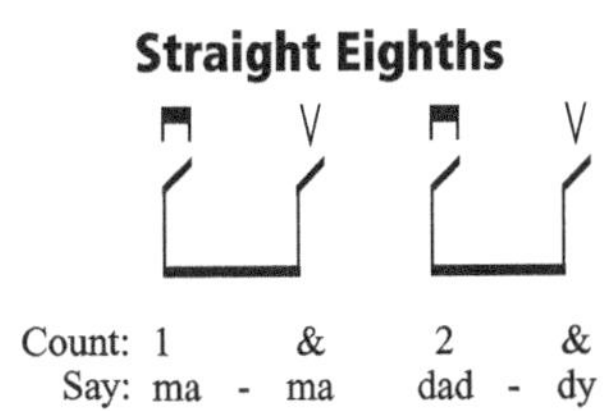

In blues and jazz, eighth notes are played unevenly and are called *swing eighths.* This rhythm is also called a *shuffle beat.* The basic beat is subdivided into three parts (triplets); the eighth note played on the downbeat receives two thirds of the beat, and the second eighth played on the upbeat receives one third of the beat: long-short, long-short.

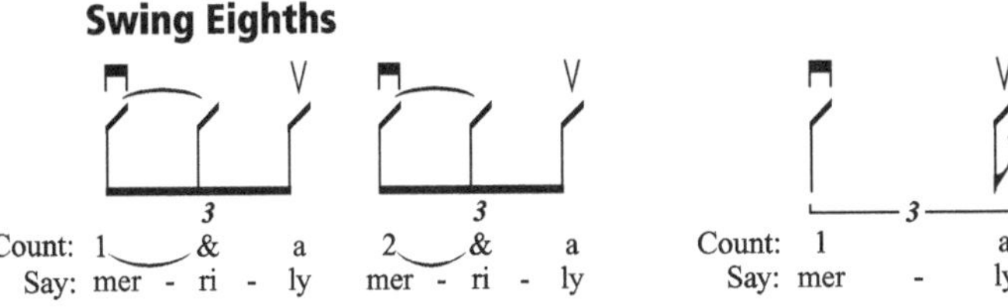

It is common practice among musicians and publishers to write music in straight eighths, and to simply indicate that they are to be performed as swing eighths.

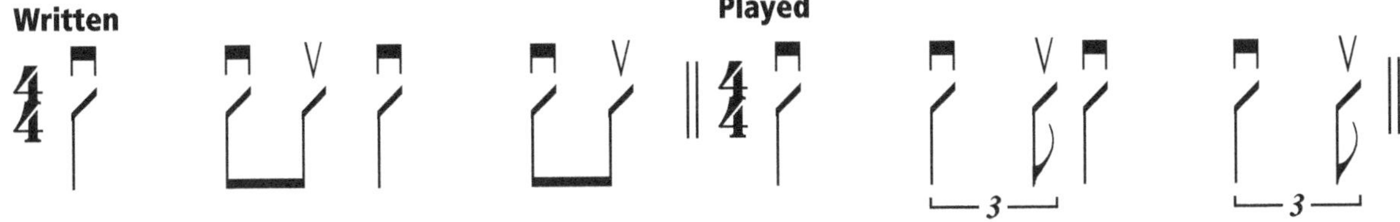

Basic Blues Strum

To play the basic blues strum, strum the chord from the root on beats 1 and 3. On beats 2 and 4, strum a down-up pattern with either a pick or the index finger (scratch). Practice example 34.

Now play "Depression Blues" using the basic blues strum.

Power Chords

Power chords first appeared in the music of Link Wray in 1958 and have since become a mainstay of the rock style. Power chords are located on the bass strings and contain only two different notes: a root and a fifth (no third). Power chords are indicated with a 5. For example, the A5 ("A five") is a chord with the root (A) and the fifth (E). In some power chord shapes, the root is doubled.

Open power chords are the easiest to play. They contain an open bass string and can be played with one finger.

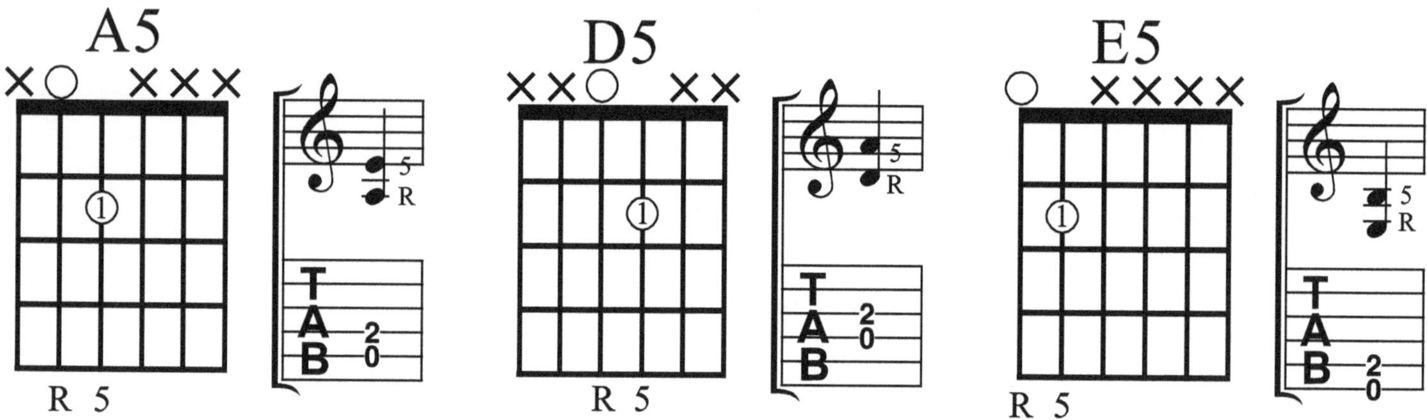

Power chords are usually played with consecutive down-strokes (straight eighths) with a pick, but fingerstyle players can play them with a scratch strum using the index finger.

CD 28

Open Five Power

By *accenting*, or stressing, certain beats, you can make this strum more interesting. Accent the notes that occur on beats **1**, 2 **&**, and **4**. Practice example 35, and then play the "Open Five Power" chord progression with accents.

35

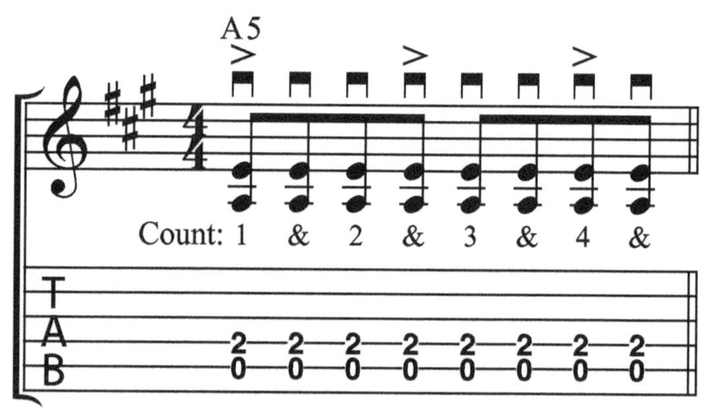

Palm Mute

The picking hand is used to *mute,* or muffle, the strings. Lightly rest the side of the hand (the heel) on the strings just in front of the bridge. If you apply too much pressure, the strings won't ring. Strum the strings with consecutive down-strokes. A pick is generally used, but you can also do this with an index finger scratch. This strum adds a nice percussive sound to rock, metal, and some blues and pop guitar styles. On the open 6th and 5th strings, practice the palm mute, and then apply it to the chord progression in "Open Five Power" on the previous page.

Open Sixth Chords

From the A5, D5, and E5 open power chords, you can move to the open A6 ("A sixth"), D6, and E6 chords with the 3rd finger of the fretting hand. When moving to the sixth chord, keep the 1st finger of the fretting hand on the 2nd fret and appropriate string of each chord.

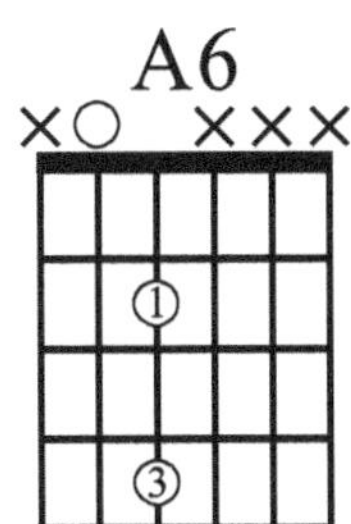

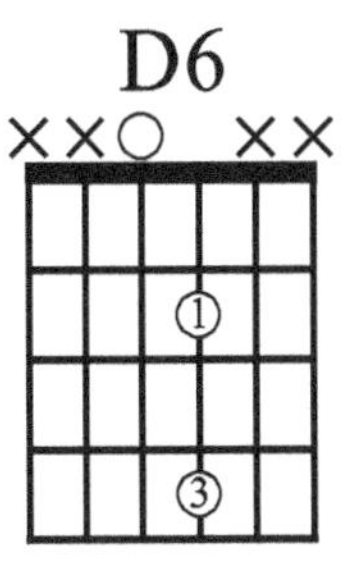

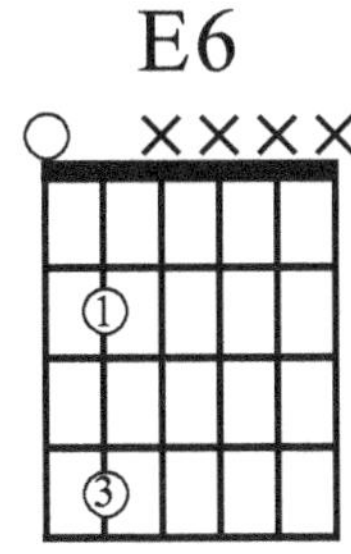

A *shuffle rhythm* is made up of consecutive swing eighths. You can play "A Blues Shuffle" several ways: 1) play it with swing eighths, 2) play it with a palm mute, 3) play in a rock style with straights eighths and a palm mute.

A Blues Shuffle

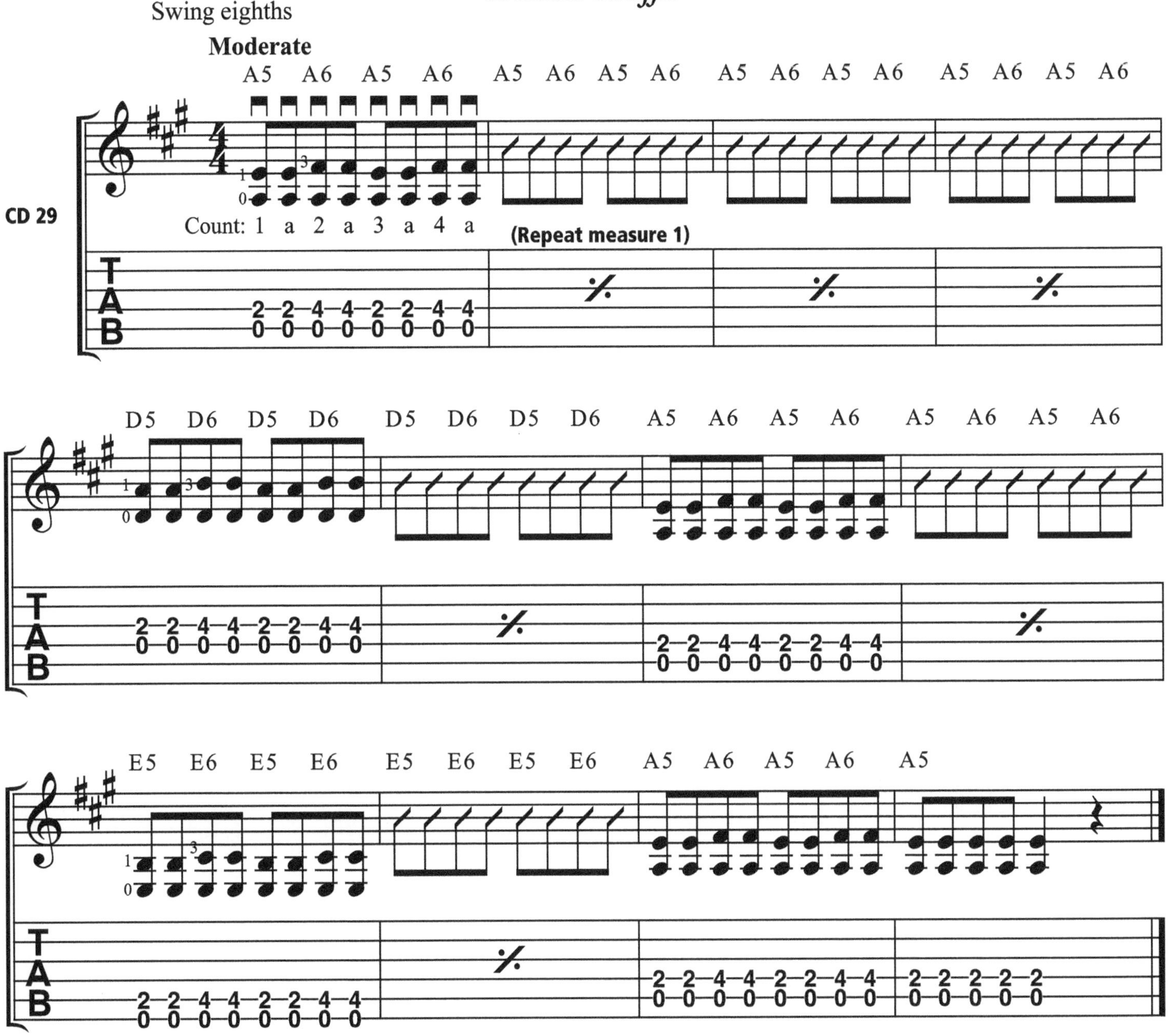

Swing eighths

Moderate

CD 29

A5 A6 A5 A6 | A5 A6 A5 A6 | A5 A6 A5 A6 | A5 A6 A5 A6

Count: 1 a 2 a 3 a 4 a

(Repeat measure 1)

D5 D6 D5 D6 | D5 D6 D5 D6 | A5 A6 A5 A6 | A5 A6 A5 A6

E5 E6 E5 E6 | E5 E6 E5 E6 | A5 A6 A5 A6 | A5

KEY OF E

> ***THEORY***
> The primary chords in the key of E are E, A, and B7. They are built upon the first, fourth, and fifth tones of the E scale.

E Scale and Primary Chords

E Chord

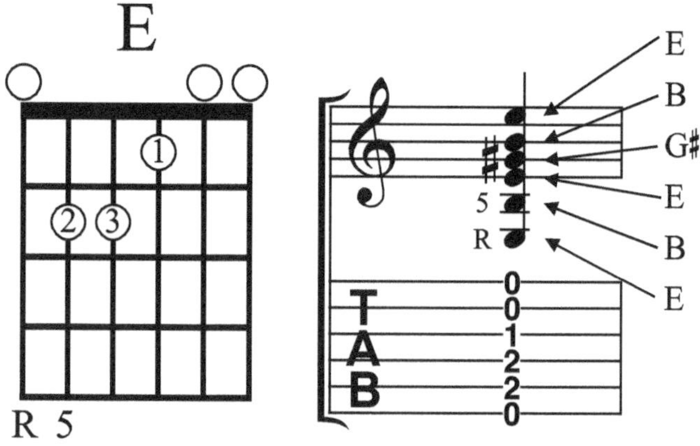

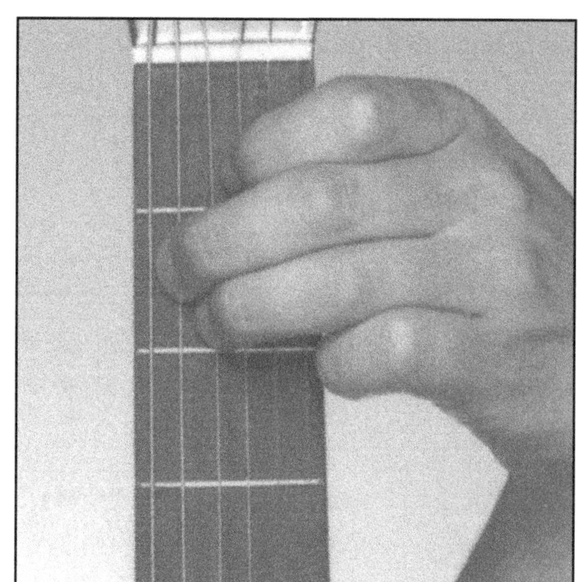

> ***THEORY***
> In the key of E, the E chord is the *tonic,* or *I chord.* The primary bass (R) is located on the open 6th string. The alternate bass (5) is located on the 5th string.

B7 Chord

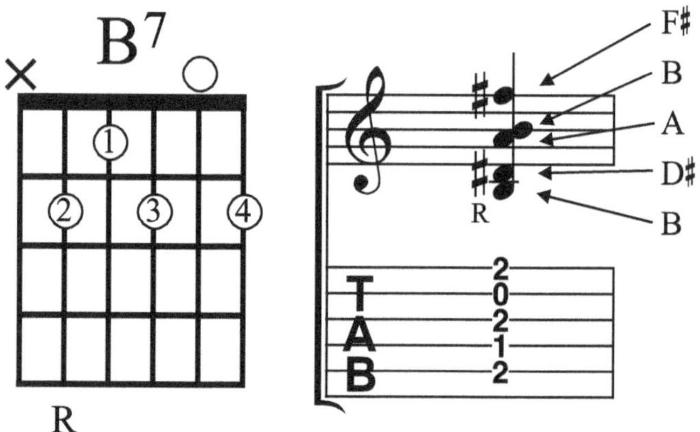

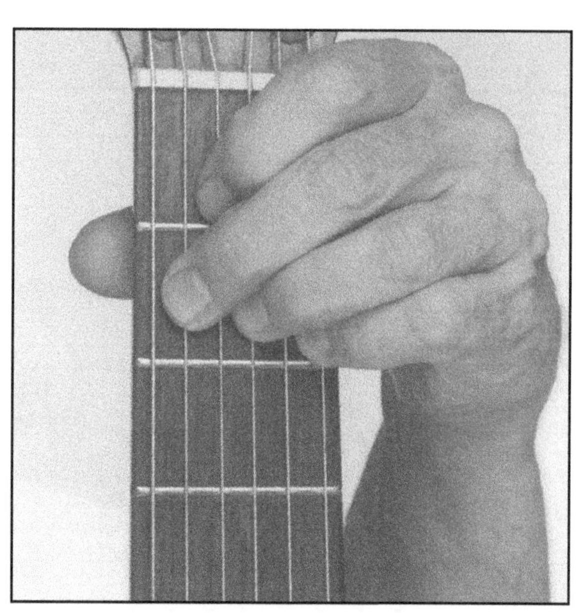

> ***THEORY***
> The B7 chord functions as the *dominant 7th,* or *V7 chord* in the key of E. The primary bass (R) is located on the 5th string, 2nd fret.

Using a pick or brush strum, practice the following drills.

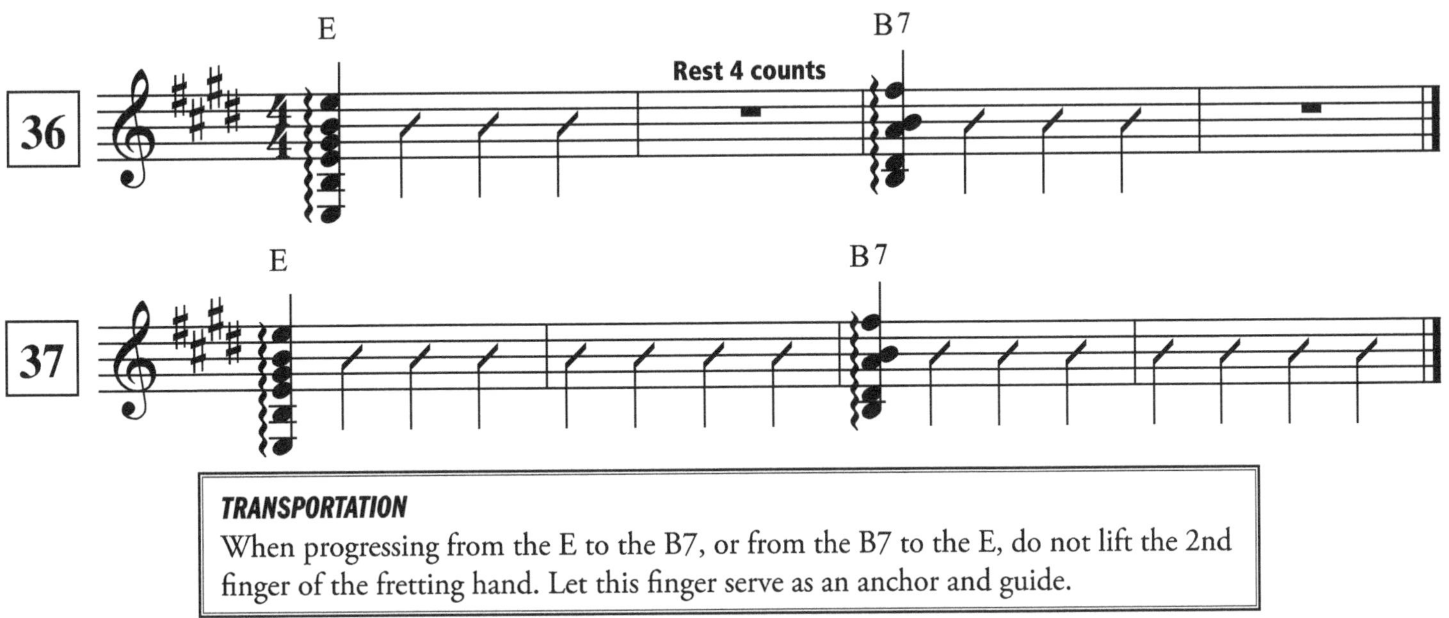

TRANSPORTATION
When progressing from the E to the B7, or from the B7 to the E, do not lift the 2nd finger of the fretting hand. Let this finger serve as an anchor and guide.

For additional practice using the E and B7 chords, transpose "Mary Ann," "Good News," and "Puttin' on the Style" into the key of E. Substitute the E and B7 chords for the D and A7 chords.

Alternate Bass (Fifth)

In the case of the B7 chord, in order to play the alternate bass (5), you must fret the 6th string at the 2nd fret. Most guitarists lift the 2nd finger of the left hand back and forth between the 5th and 6th strings.

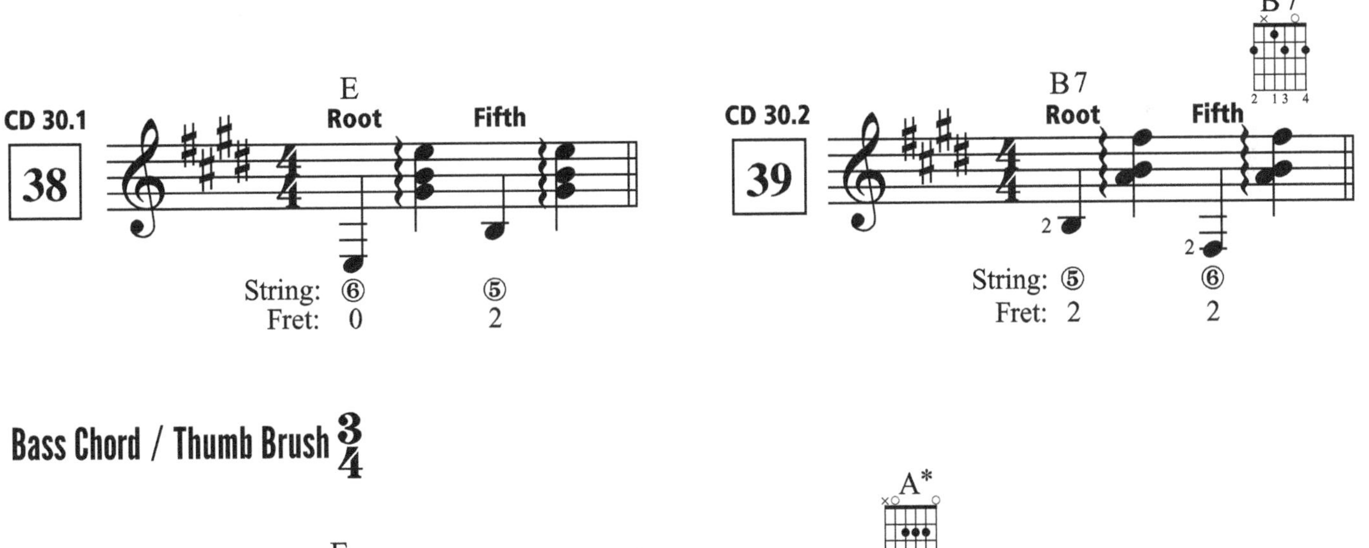

Bass Chord / Thumb Brush $\frac{3}{4}$

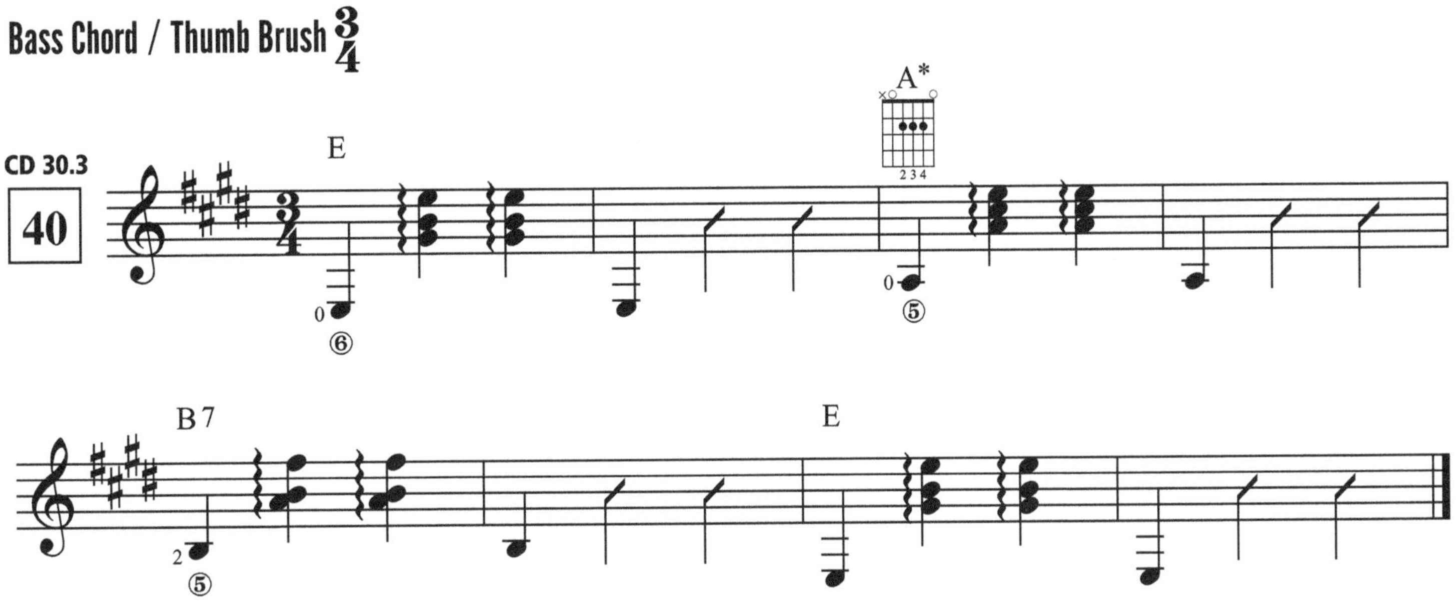

*Try using optional fingering.

Amazing Grace

Traditional

CD 31
First Note

Slowly

E A E

1. A - maz - ing grace, how sweet the sound that
2. 'Twas grace that taught my heart to fear, and
3. Through man - y dan - gers, toil and snares I

B7

saved a wretch like me! I
grace my fears re - lieved. How
have al - read - y come. 'Tis

E A E

once was lost but now am found; was
pre - cious did that grace ap - pear the
grace hath brought me safe thus far and

B7 E

blind, but now I see.
hour I first be - lieved.
grace will lead me home.

Hush, Little Baby

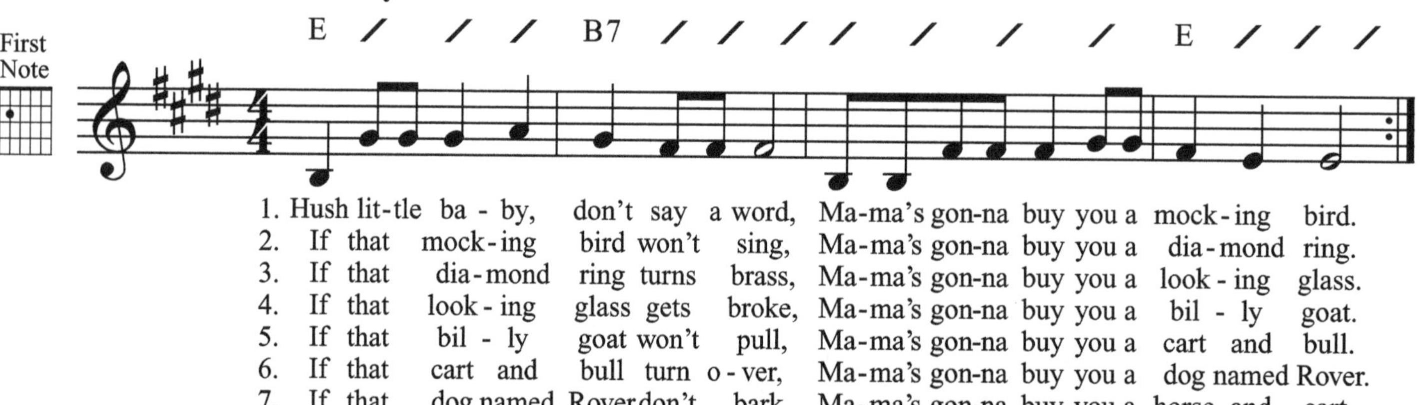

Mute

The *mute* is a picking hand technique in which the strings are *dampened* (silenced) immediately following a down-stroke with a pick or a scratch strum. Strum downward across the strings, from bass to treble, and then mute the strings by rolling onto the side of the hand or by simply collapsing the hand downward onto the strings. This should be done in **one continuous** downward motion. The primary motion is downward and into the strings.

Practice several mutes in a row on open strings. Strive for a "chunk" sound with silence between each mute.

CD 32.1

41

mute silence mute silence mute silence mute silence

Count: 1 2 3 4

In example 42, strum the strings on beats 1 and 3, mute the strings with an accent (>) on beats 2 and 4. The chord pattern should sound like "chord-chunk-silence."

CD 32.2

42

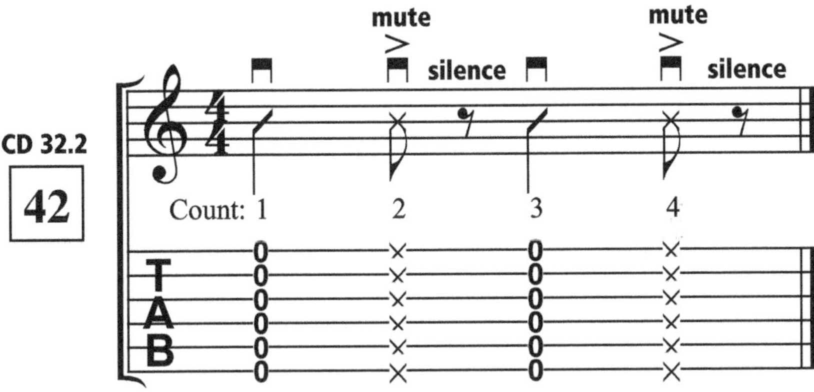

Add an up-stroke with a pick or a scratch strum on beats 1**a** and 3**a** for example 43. You only need to strum the treble strings. Play swing eighths, as shown below.

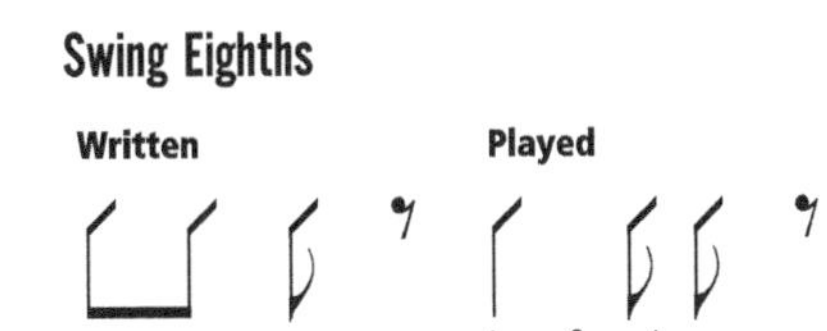

CD 32.3

43

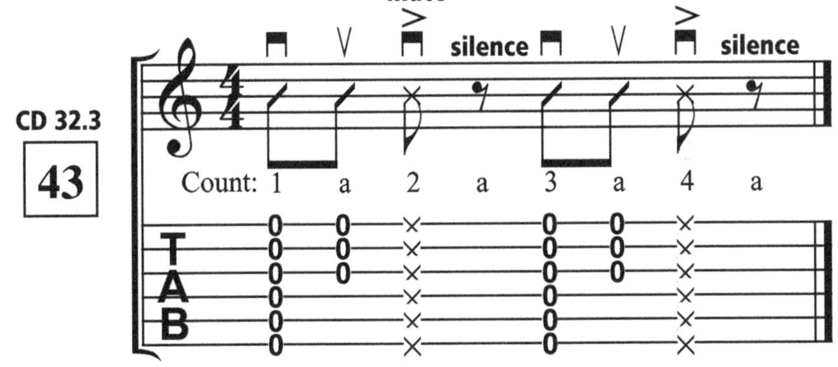

Blues Strum

Now add an up-stroke to beats 2**a** and 4**a** in chord example 44. Play swing eighths (shuffle rhythm). Then, apply the blues strum to "C. C. Rider" and "Bricks in My Pillow."

CD 32.4

44

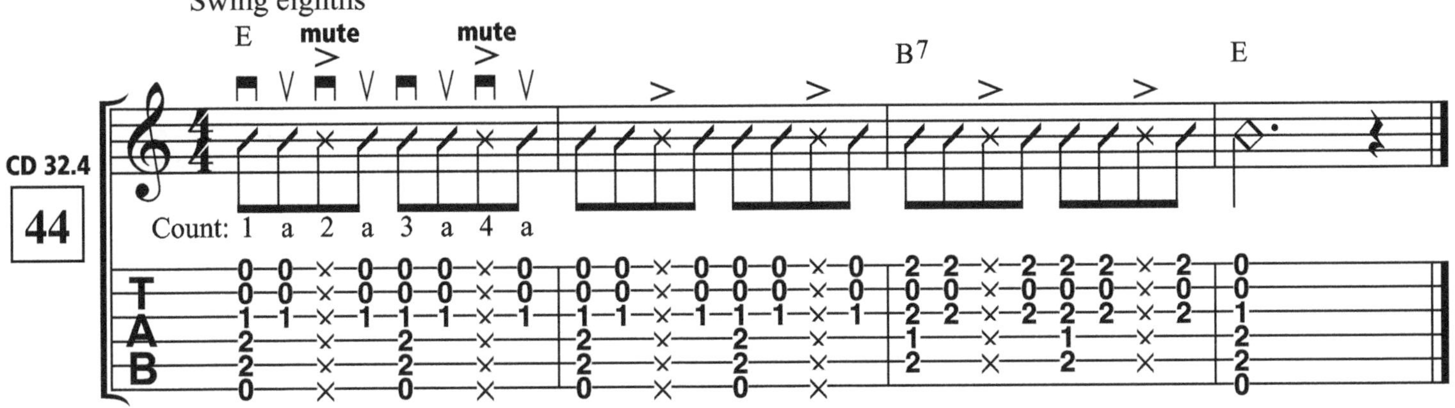

C. C. Rider
Traditional
Slowly
Blues Strum
(continue pattern)
First Note
E
E7
1. C. C. Ri-der, look at what you done. Oh
2. Sun - shine Spe-cial com - in' 'round the bend. That
3. C. C. Ri-der, you have made me cry. Yes,
A7*
C. C. Ri - der, look at what you done. You
Sun - shine Spe - cial com - in' 'round the bend. Has
C. C. Ri - der, you have made me cry. You've
1st & 2nd Ending
3rd Ending
1.2.
3.
B7
made me love you, now your sweet-heart's come.
got your wo - man, now our love must end.
got me feel - in' like I want to die.
TRANSPORTATION
Use the alternate A7 fingering to eliminate unnecessary fretting hand movement.
*A7
(alternate fingering)
(5) R 5
Bricks in My Pillow
CD 33
Traditional
Slowly
1. I've got bricks in my pil - low and my head can't rest no more.
2. I've got holes in my pock - ets great big patch - es on my pants.
I've got bricks in my pil - low and my head can't rest no more.
I've got holes in my pock - ets great big patch - es on my pants.
Spi - ders crawl - in' on my walls, blacksnakes ly - ing on my floor.
I'm be - hind with my house rent, land - lord wants it in ad - vance.

KEY OF E MINOR

The melody and chords in the key of Em (E minor) are based on the E harmonic minor scale. The Em chord assumes the role of "home base."

> ***THEORY***
> The primary chords in the key of Em are Em, Am, and B7. They are constructed on the first, fourth, and fifth tones of the E harmonic minor scale (the seventh note is raised one half step).

E Harmonic Minor Scale and Primary Chords

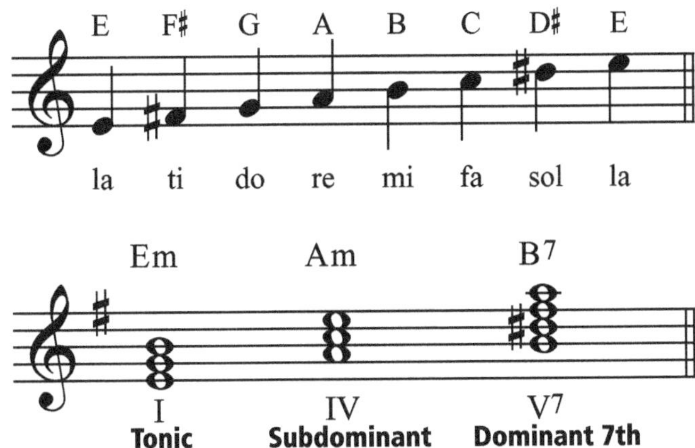

Em Chord

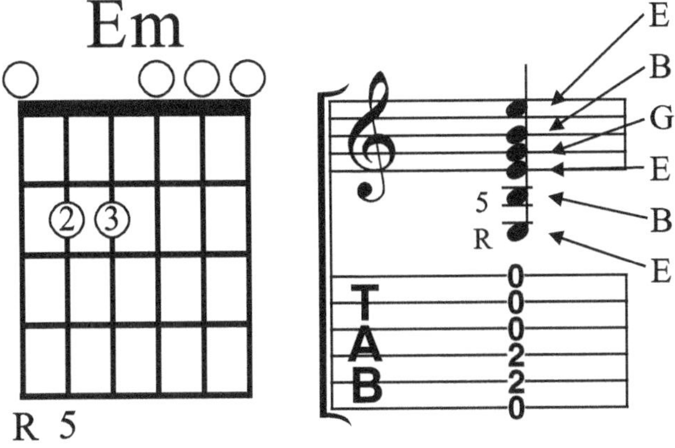

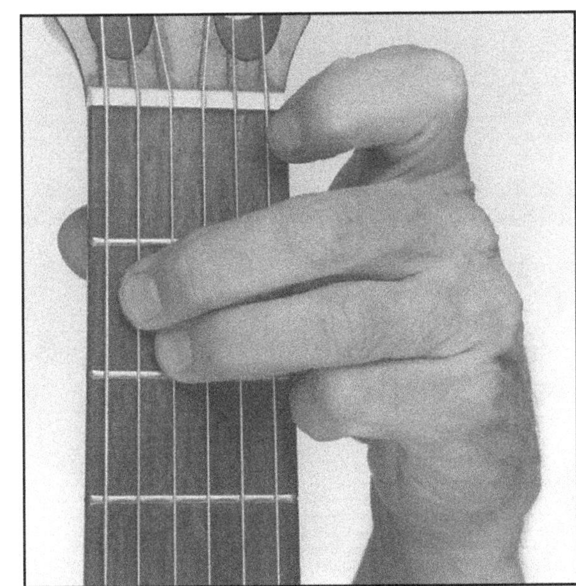

> ***THEORY***
> The Em chord is the *tonic,* or *I chord.* Its primary bass (R) is located on the open 6th string. The alternate bass (5) is located on the 5th string, 2nd fret.

Am Chord

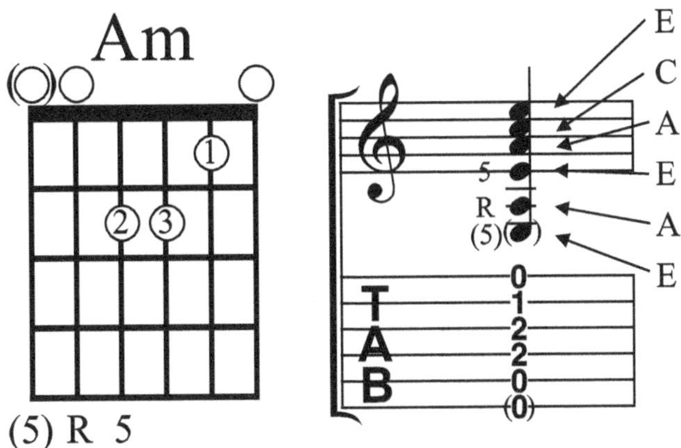

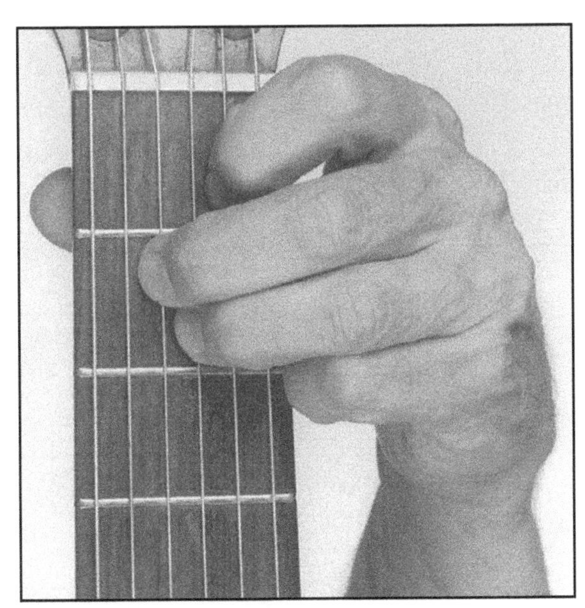

> ***THEORY***
> The Am chord is the *subdominant,* or *IV chord.* The primary bass (R) is the open 5th string. The alternate bass (5) is on the open 6th string, or the 4th string, 2nd fret.

Using a pick or a brush strum, practice the following drill until you can make the changes smoothly and without hesitation. When going from the B7 to the Em chord, do not lift the 2nd finger of the fretting hand. The 2nd finger functions as a guide finger.

45

Em
2 3
Am
2 3 1
B7
2 1 3 4
Em
2 3

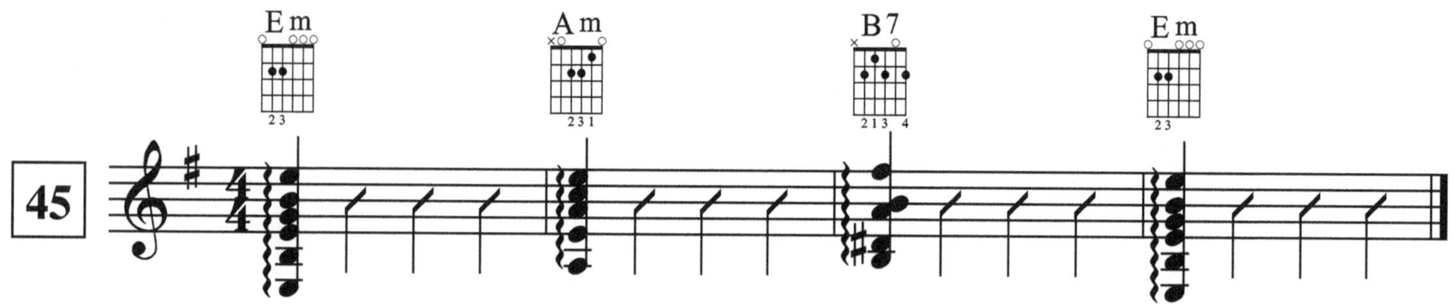

Alternate Bass (Fifth)

Alternate the pick or thumb between the primary bass (R) and alternate bass (5) of the Em and Am chords.

46

Em
Root
Fifth
String: ⑥ ⑤
Fret: 0 2

47

Am
Root
Fifth
Root
Fifth
String: ⑤ ⑥ ⑤ ④
Fret: 0 0 0 2

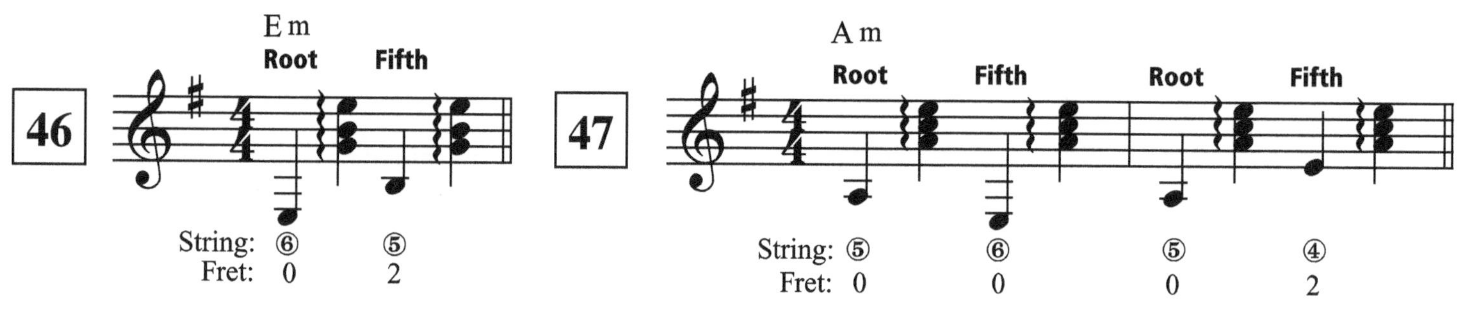

This Old Hammer

Work Song (adapted)

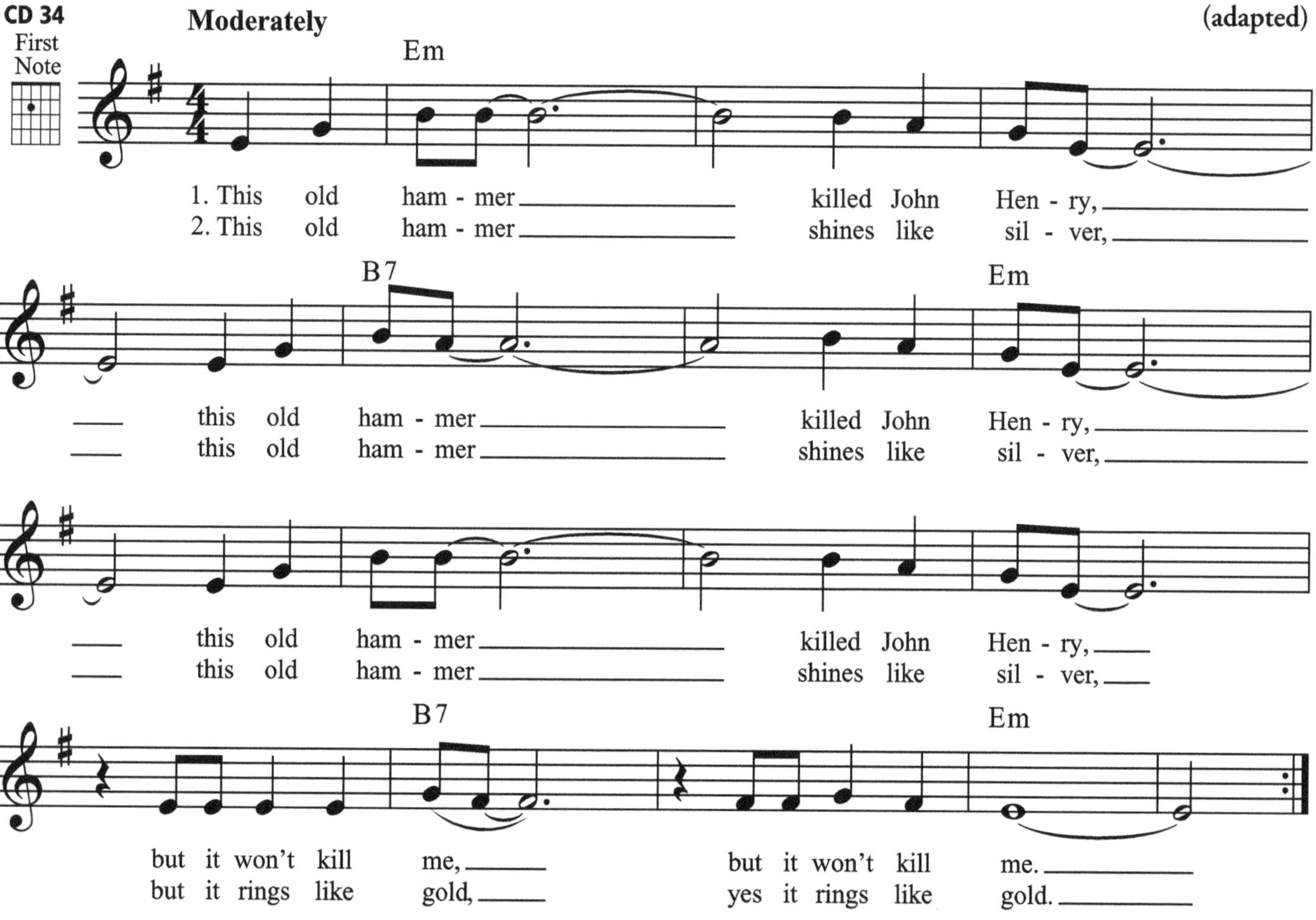

CD 34
First Note
Moderately
Em
1. This old ham - mer killed John Hen - ry,
2. This old ham - mer shines like sil - ver,
B7
Em
this old ham - mer killed John Hen - ry,
this old ham - mer shines like sil - ver,
this old ham - mer killed John Hen - ry,
this old ham - mer shines like sil - ver,
B7
Em
but it won't kill me, but it won't kill me.
but it rings like gold, yes it rings like gold.

St. Louis Blues

W.C. Handy

KEY OF C

In the key of C, the C chord functions as the tonal center, or "home base." The C scale serves as the skeleton upon which the melodies and harmonies are constructed.

C Scale and Primary Chords

> ***THEORY***
> The primary chords in the key of C are C, F, and G7. They are built on the first, fourth, and fifth tones of the C scale.

G7 Chord

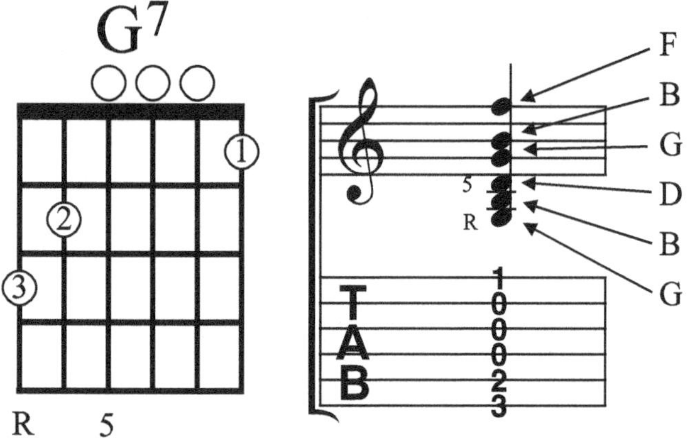

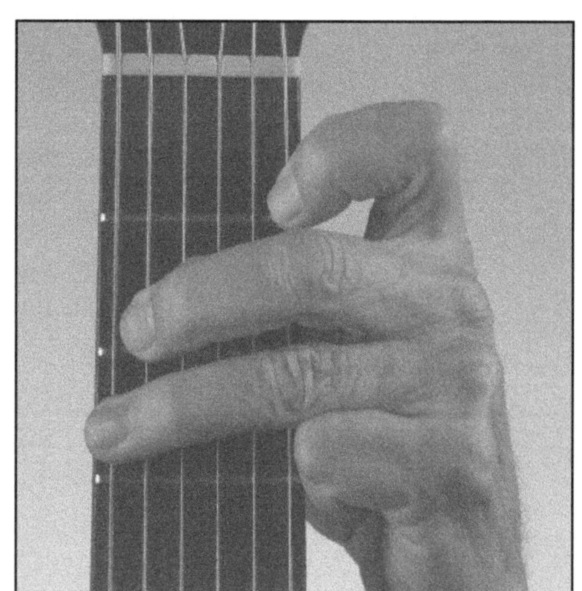

> ***THEORY***
> The G7 chord is the *dominant 7th,* or *V7 chord* in the key of C. The primary bass (R) is located on the 6th string, 3rd fret. The alternate bass (5) is located on the open 4th string.

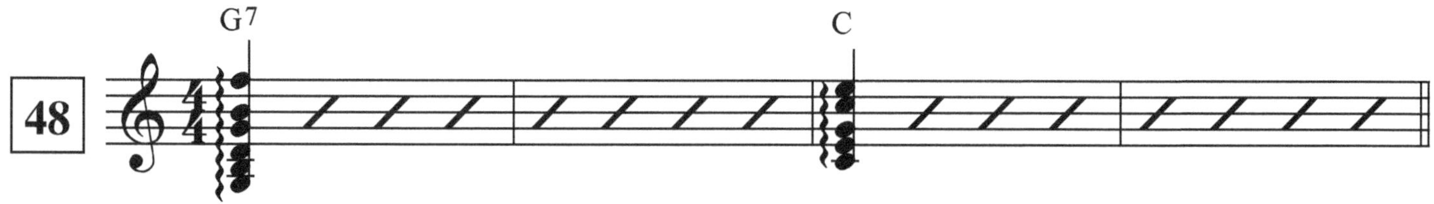

> ***TRANSPORTATION***
> Notice the similarity in shape between the C and G7 chords. The fingers of the fretting hand are in relatively the same shape. Think of the G7 chord as an expanded C chord.

For additional practice using the C and G7 chords, transpose "Some Folks Do," "Good News," and "He's Got the Whole World in His Hands" from the key of D to the key of C.

Pay Me My Money Down

Traditional

CD 36

First Note

C G7

I thought I heard the cap - tain say pay me my mon - ey down. To -

C

mor - row is our sail - ing day. Pay me my mon - ey down.

Chorus:

C G7

Pay me, oh, pay me, pay me my mon - ey down

C

pay me or go to jail, pay me my mon - ey down.

Now the Day Is Over

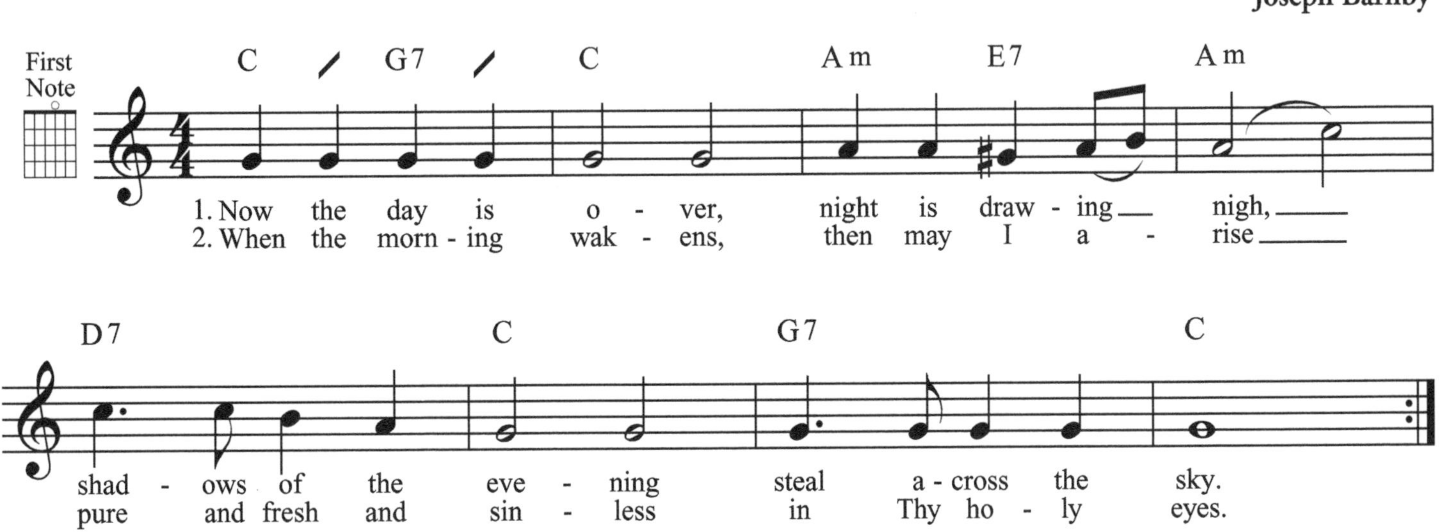

Thumb Sweep

In the *thumb sweep*, the thumb (*p*) strums, or sweeps, downward (⊓) across the strings from low to high. The sweep most often begins with the root (R) of the chord, Keep the thumb rigid.

Calypso Strum

The *calypso strum* uses a combination of the brush, sweep, and scratch strums. **Brush down** across the strings on beat **1**, **sweep down** across the strings on 1 **&**, **scratch up** on **2**, **brush down** on 2 **&** with emphasis, and then **scratch up-down-up** on **& 4 &**.

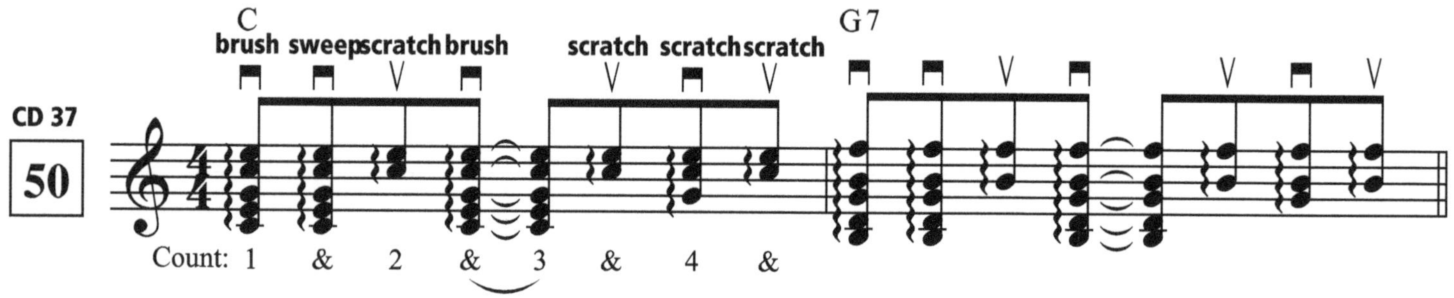

Traditional

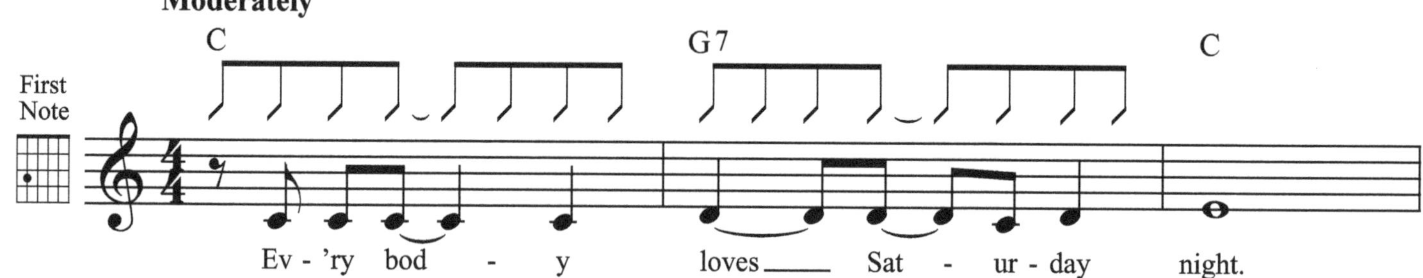

In the following calypso strum, it is necessary to change to the C chord on the upbeat of 2 **&**.
Apply this strum to "Banana Boat Song."

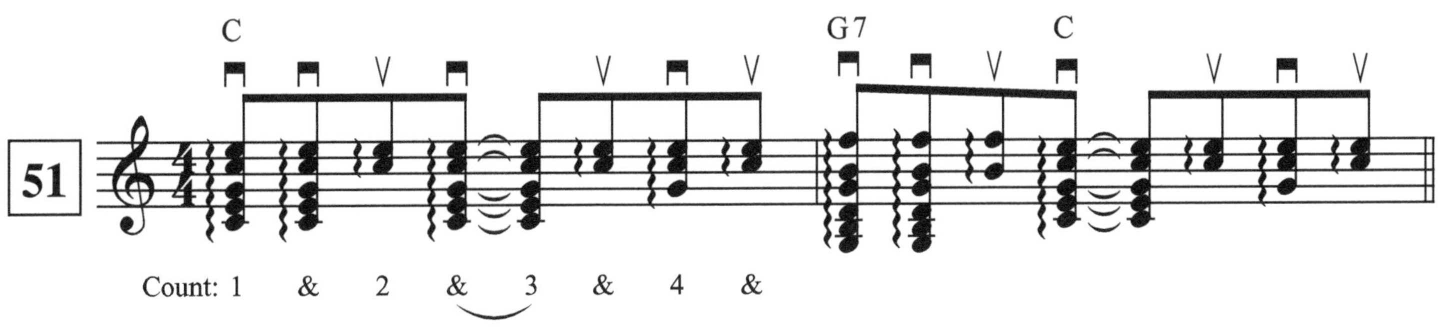

Banana Boat Song

Jamaican Folk Song

Moderately

CD 38
First Note

C
Calypso Strum *(continue pattern)*

C ... G7 C
Day ___ oh! ___ Day ___ oh! ___ Day - light come ___ an' I wan-na go home. ___

C ... G7 C
Day ___ oh! ___ Day ___ oh! ___ Day - light come ___ an' I wan-na go home. ___

C ... G7 C
Work on ba - na - na boat all day long. Day - light come ___ an' I wan-na go home. ___
Stuff ba - na-nas til de morn - in' come. Day - light come ___ an' I wan-na go home. ___

C ... G7 C
Day ___ oh! ___ Day ___ oh! ___ Day - light come ___ an' I wan-na go home. ___

C ... G7 ... C ... G7 C
Come Mis-ter tal - ly man, tal - ly me ba - na - na. Day - light come ___ an' I wan-na go home. ___

C ... G7 C
Day ___ oh! ___ Day ___ oh! ___ Day - light come ___ an' I wan-na go home. ___

F Chord

The F chord is more difficult to play than any of the previous chords because it requires the 1st finger of the fretting hand to *fret* (cover) more than one string. Guitarists and teachers approach this problem in a variety of ways, and, as a result, there are many versions and fingerings of the F chord: three-string version, four-string version, five-string version, six-string version with grand bar, and six-string version using the thumb.

Small Bar

When the 1st finger is used to fret more than one string at a time, it is called *barring.* If two, three, or four strings are fretted at the same time, it is called a *small bar* or *half bar.* One version of the F chord is the small bar F chord.

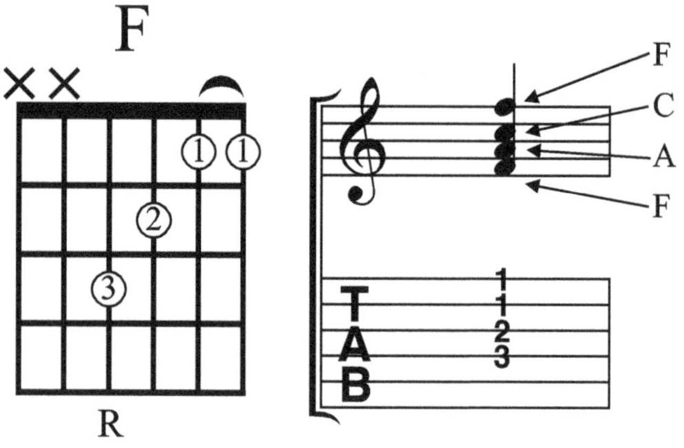

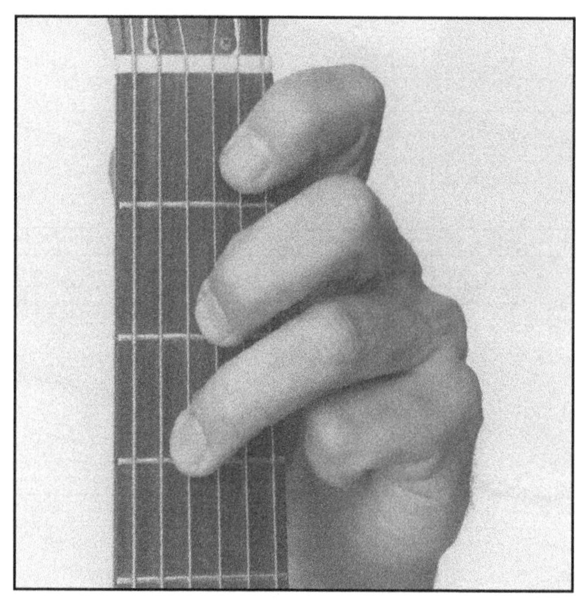

THEORY

The F chord is built on the fourth degree of the C scale and is the *subdominant,* or *IV chord.* The primary bass is located on the 4th string, 3rd fret.

Begin by developing the ability to play a small bar, as in step 1 below. Since more pressure is necessary at the 1st fret, try practicing the small bar technique at the 5th and 3rd frets. When you can successfully cover the 1st and 2nd strings with the index finger, progress to steps 2 and 3.

Step 1: The index finger covers the 1st and 2nd strings. To avoid a "buzz," fret the string close to the metal fret dividers. The pressure should be applied to the outer edge of the finger.

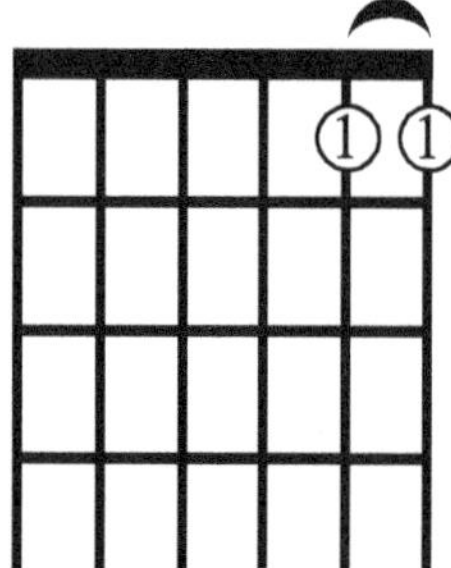

Step 2: Now add the 2nd finger to the chord. Avoid touching the 1st and 2nd strings with the 2nd finger. Fingernails must be short.

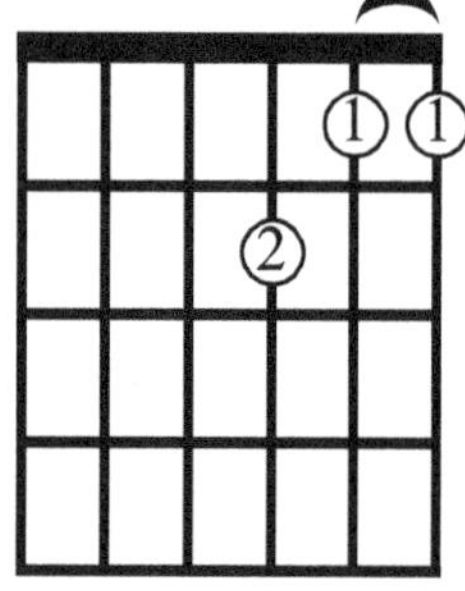

Step 3: Next, add the 3rd finger. Be careful not to touch the 3rd string with the 3rd finger. Because the string *action* is generally higher at the 1st fret of the guitar, it is easier to develop the small bar technique on higher frets. Keep the wrist straight and the palm of the hand away from the neck of the guitar.

Another approach is to begin with a three-string version of the F chord and eventually add the small bar.

Deaden the 1st string (X) by lightly touching it with the inside of the index finger. This simplified three-string F chord should eventually be replaced with the small bar.

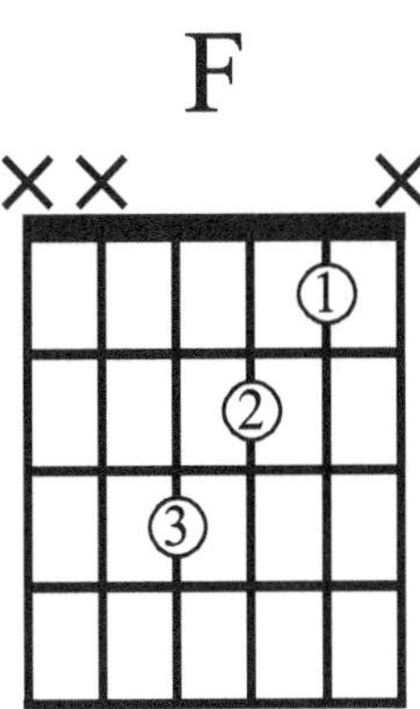

Alternate Bass (Fifth)

Two methods may be used to play the alternate bass (5) when using the small bar F chord.

Method 1. Move the 3rd finger back and forth between the 4th and 5th strings. This form leaves the 4th finger "free" for playing melody notes.

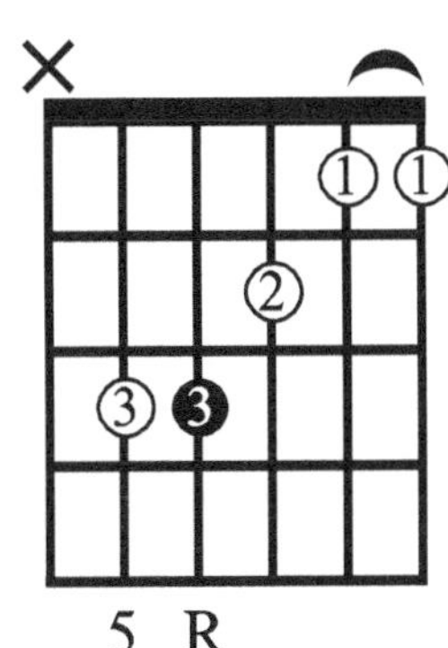

Method 2. This five-string version of the F chord allows you to play the alternate bass without moving the fingers.

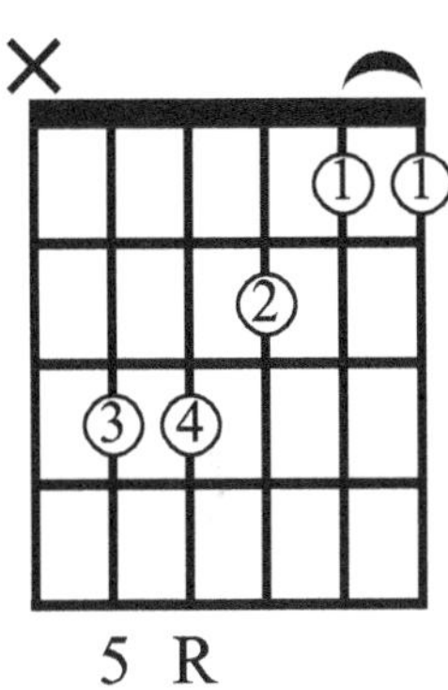

52

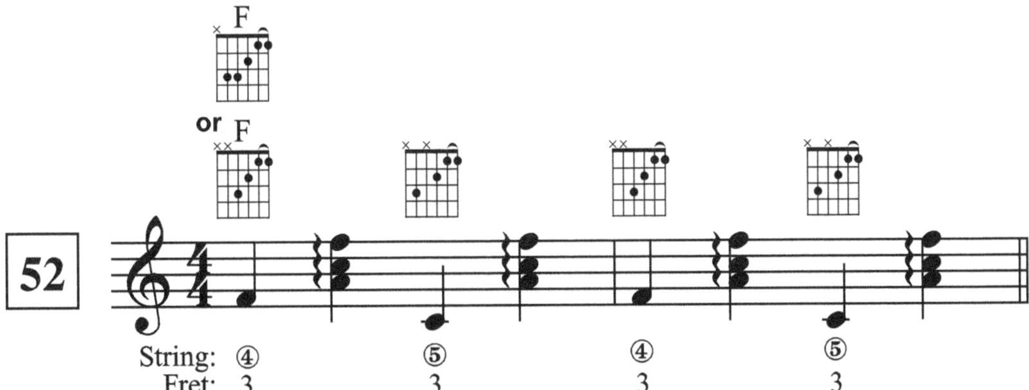

CD 39.1

53

> ***TRANSPORTATION***
> When changing from the C to the F chord, do not lift the 2nd finger—simply roll the finger into the small bar position.

Example 54 is a suggested accompaniment for "Oh, Danny Boy."
Alternate the bass between the root and the fifth of the chords on beats 1 and 3.

Grand Bar

Unfortunately, the ability to play the small bar F chord does little to prepare you for the problems presented by the *grand bar*, or *full bar*, F chord. For the grand bar, you must cover all six strings and often use the 4th finger to fret various strings.

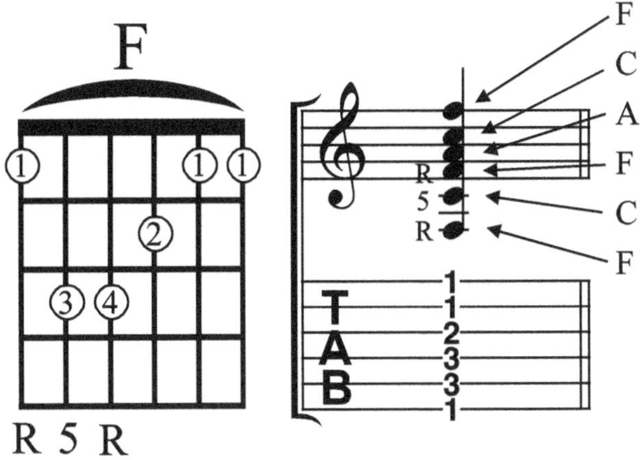

THEORY
The primary bass (R) is located on either the 4th string, 3rd fret, or the 6th string, 1st fret. The alternate bass (5) is located on the 5th string, 3rd fret.

Begin developing the ability to play the grand bar with step 1 below. Because of the height of the strings at the 1st fret and the distance between frets, it is recommended that you first apply the grand bar at the **5th fret** and gradually work your way down to the 1st fret. Then progress to steps 2 and 3.

Step 1: The index finger must be as straight as possible from the tip to the knuckle. The wrist is straight with the thumb placed opposite the index finger (grip position). The palm of the hand must not touch the neck of the guitar.

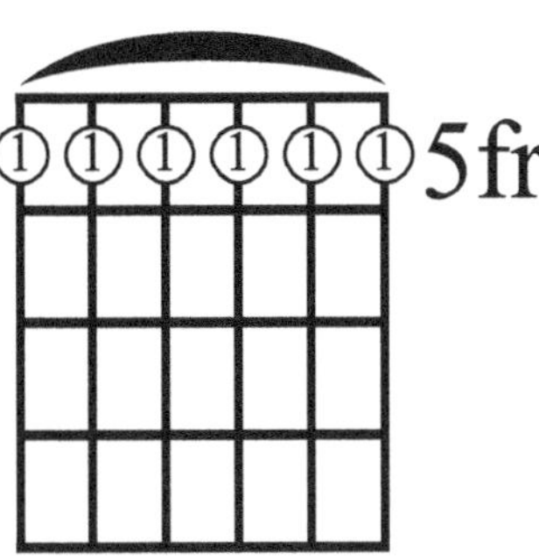

Step 2: Now add the 2nd and 3rd fingers to the chord. This is actually a dominant 7th chord form of the bar chord. The 3rd finger should not touch the 4th string.

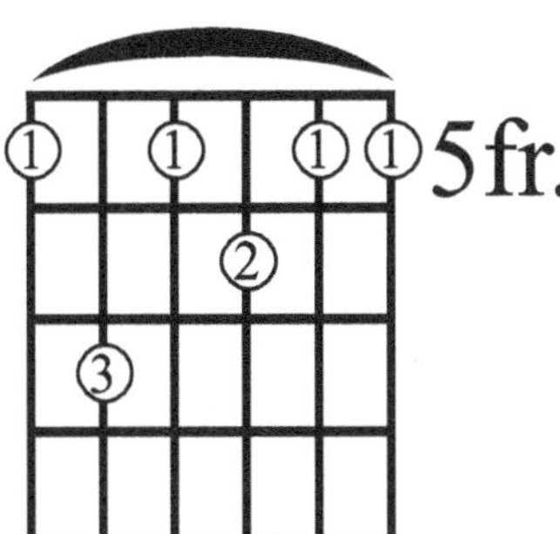

Step 3: Add the 4th finger to complete the chord.

Thumb Option

In many styles of guitar, the use of the thumb to aid in fretting chords is frowned upon. There are, however, some legitimate reasons for using the thumb, such as when playing very involved jazz chords, some country styles (finger-picking), bluegrass, and ragtime, that require use of the thumb to solve particular fingering problems. Using the thumb should not be used as a solution for one's inability to play bar chords, however. The thumb option fingering is presented here so that you will understand its use; it is not recommended at this stage.

This form is most often used on a flat-top or electric guitar that has a narrow neck. It is more difficult to play on a nylon string folk or classic guitar.

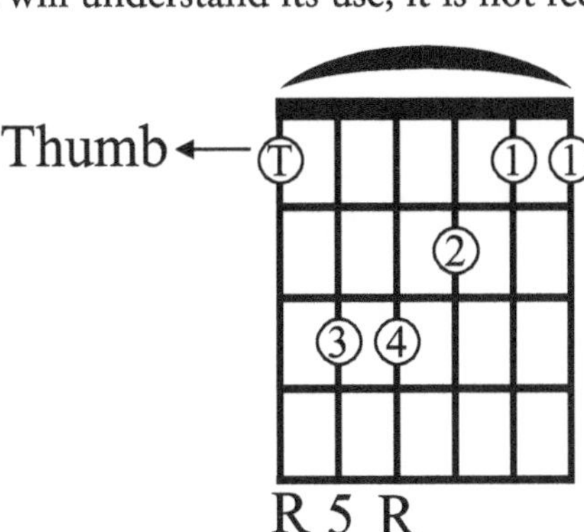

Hard, Ain't It Hard
Traditional
CD 41
First Note
Brightly
C F
It's hard, ain't it hard, ain't it hard to
C G7
love one who nev - er will love you. It's
C F
hard and it's hard, ain't it hard, great God, to
C G7 C
love one who nev - er will be true.
John Hardy
Bluegrass
First Note
Lively
F C
Well now John Har - dy was a des - p'rate lit - tle man, he
F C F
car - ried a ra - zor ev - 'ry day, he killed a man on the
C G7
West Vir - gin - ia line. You ought'a see John Har - dy get - tin' a -
C
way, ought'a see John Har - dy get - ting a - way.

Fingerstyle Free Strokes

The index finger (*i*), middle finger (*m*), and ring finger (*a*) of the fretting hand will now be used to play guitar accompaniment by plucking the strings simultaneously, individually, or in a combination of the two. In classical guitar, this stroke is called a *tirando.*

Plant the fingers on the strings as follows:

1. index finger (*i* = indice) on the 3rd string (G)
2. middle finger (*m* = medio) on the 2nd string (B)
3. ring finger (*a* = anular) on the 1st string (E)

Bunch the fingers together with the tips touching the strings close to the fingernails.

Hand position, fingers curved.

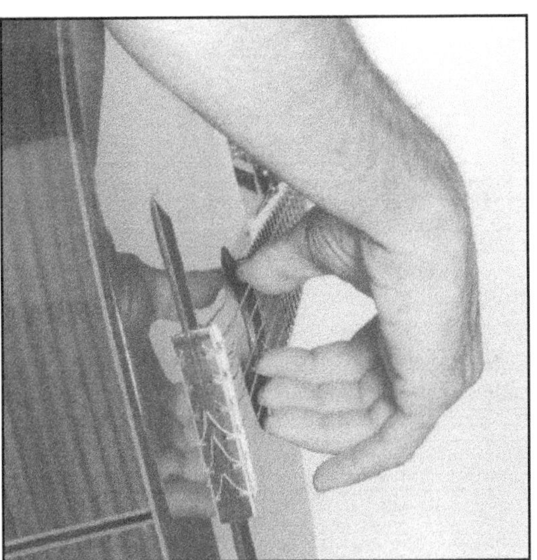

Hand position, thumb extended.

When playing the *free stroke*, the fingers do not come to rest on the adjacent string. After plucking the strings, the fingers pass over the neighboring lower-pitched strings. The primary motion is with the fingers and comes from the knuckle nearest the hand. Do not raise the hand; simply curl the fingers into it. The forearm should remain in position above the bridge base.

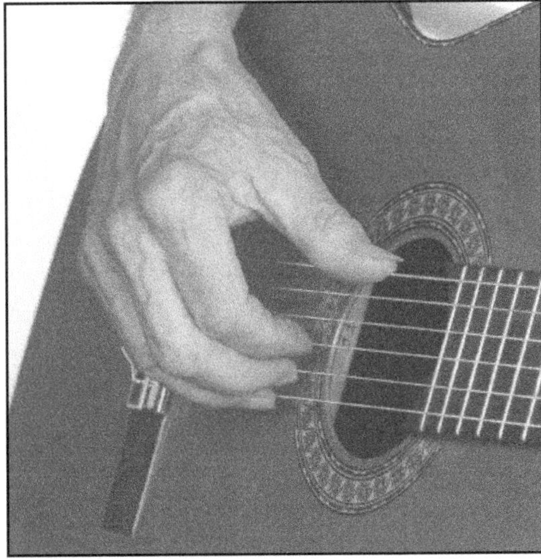

Free stroke, preparation.

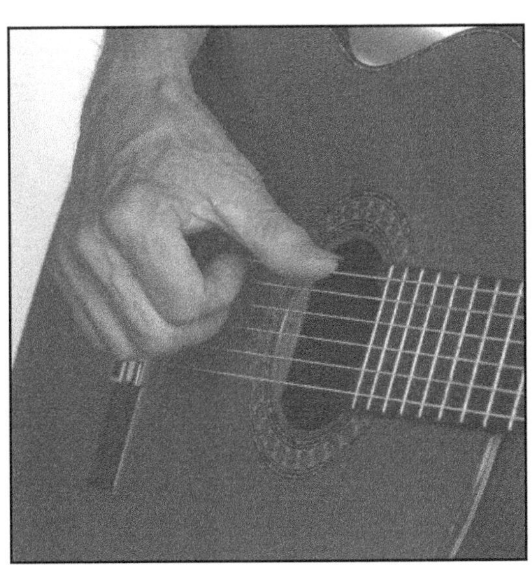

Free stroke, completion.

Bass Chord / Thumb Pluck $\frac{3}{4}$

The pickstyle *bass chord* $\frac{3}{4}$ pattern is performed by plucking the root of the chord with a pick and then strumming the treble strings twice using down-strokes. The fingerstyle *thumb pluck* $\frac{3}{4}$ pattern is performed by plucking the root of the chord with the thumb and then plucking the treble strings with the fingers (*i m a*). Think of your fingers as "pushing" the strings. Use *free strokes* with the thumb and fingers.

Streets of Laredo

CD 42

First Note

D (Em)* A7 (F#m) D (Em) A7
As I___ walked out in the streets of La - re - do, as

D (Em) A7 (F#m) D (Em) A7
I___ walked out in La - re - do one day, I

D (Em) A7 (F#m) D (Em) A7
spied a young cow - boy wrapped up in white lin - en, wrapped

D G A7 D
up in white lin - en as cold as the clay.

*The chords in parentheses indicate an alternate chord progression.

In example 56, it is not necessary to fret any strings for the Em chord. The F#m may be simplified by barring the 2nd fret, since the 4th and 5th strings are not plucked.

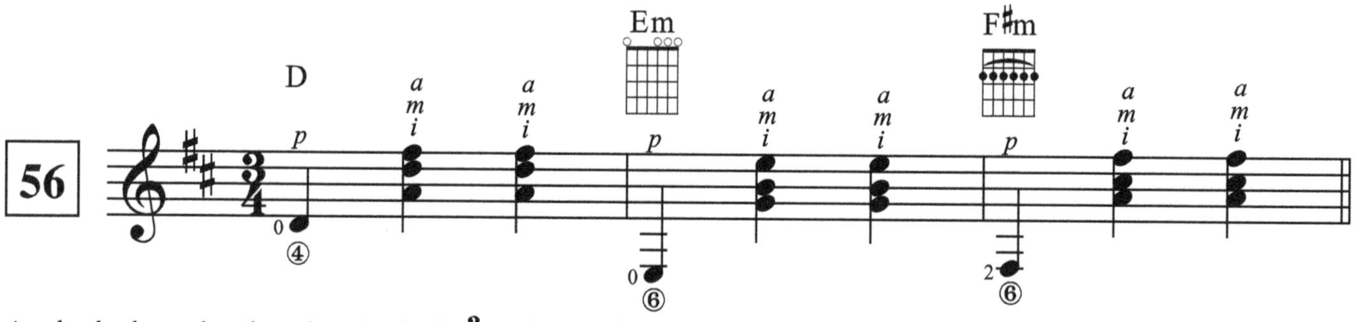

Apply the bass chord or thumb pluck $\frac{3}{4}$ to "Beautiful Brown Eyes" on page 16.

Bass Chord / Thumb Pluck $\frac{4}{4}$

For the pickstyle *bass chord* $\frac{4}{4}$ pattern, pluck the root of the chord on beats 1 and 3, and strum the chord on beats 2 and 4. Alternating to the fifth of the chord on beat 3 is optional. For the fingerstyle *thumb pluck* $\frac{4}{4}$ pattern, the thumb plucks the root of the chord, then the fingers (*i m a*) pluck the 3rd, 2nd, and 1st strings simultaneously.

Apply the bass chord or thumb pluck to "Banks of the Ohio" on page 18. Add to the accompaniment by alternating to the fifth of the chord on beat 3 .

Broken Chord / Plucking Arpeggio $\frac{3}{4}$

For the *broken chord* or *plucking arpeggio* $\frac{3}{4}$ pattern, each tone in the chord is plucked individually. In *pickstyle*, a sweep technique can be used to play each tone with one pick direction. In *fingerstyle*, the thumb (*p*) plucks the root of the chord, the index finger (*i*) plucks the 3rd string, the middle finger (*m*) plucks the 2nd string, and the ring finger (*a*) plucks the 1st string.

The broken chord and plucking arpeggio $\frac{3}{4}$ work well with "Amazing Grace" on page 36. You can also alternate the bass between the root and the fifth of the chord.

Broken Chord / Plucking Arpeggio $\frac{4}{4}$

Use all down-strokes to play the pickstyle *broken chord* $\frac{4}{4}$ pattern. As an option, try using an up-pick for all notes played on the 3rd string. In the fingerstyle *plucking arpeggio* $\frac{4}{4}$ pattern, the thumb plucks the root of the chord and may alternate to the fifth on beat 3. The index finger (*i*) plucks the 3rd string, and the middle finger (*m*) and ring finger (*a*) pluck the 2nd and 1st strings together. Give emphasis to the first and third beats of the measure. A *hybrid technique* using a combination of pick and finger technique is to pluck the 2nd and 1st strings with the middle and ring fingers, and pluck all other notes in the chord with the pick.

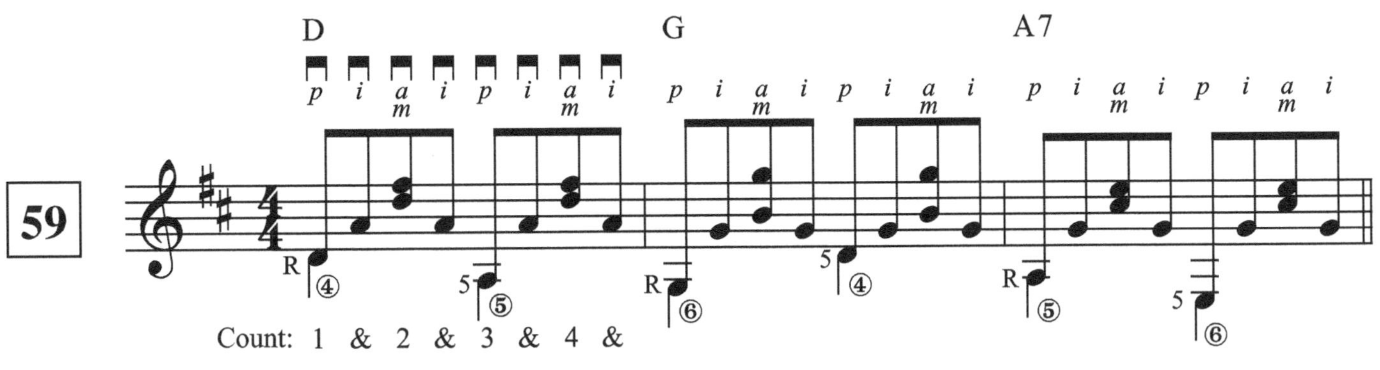

Example 60 is the alternate chord progression from "Children, Go Where I Send Thee." It is not necessary to fret any strings for the Em chord, and the F♯m can be simplified by barring the 2nd fret.

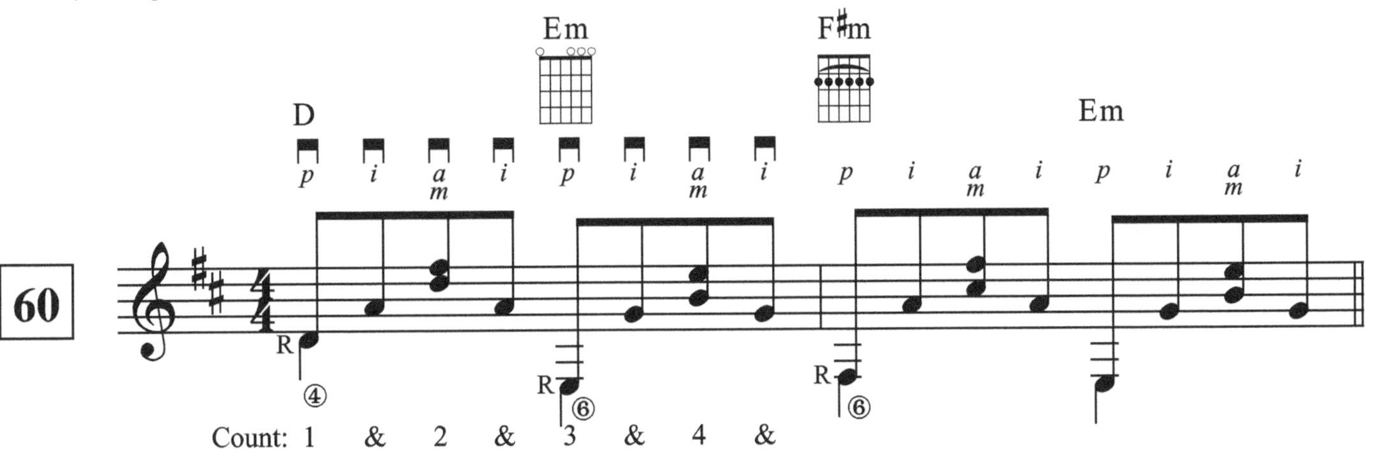

Broken Chord / Plucking Arpeggio $\frac{3}{4}$

In the broken chord or plucking arpeggio $\frac{3}{4}$ patterns, each tone in the chord is plucked individually. In pickstyle, a sweep technique can be used to play each tone with one pick direction. Practice the picking pattern indicated below (four down-strokes and two up-strokes). In fingerstyle, the thumb (*p*) plucks the root of the chord, the index finger (*i*) plucks the 3rd string, the middle finger (*m*) plucks the 2nd string, and the ring finger (*a*) plucks the 1st string.

61

Em
p i m a m i
D
p i m a m i
C
p i m a m i
B7
p i m a m i
Count: 1 & 2 & 3 &

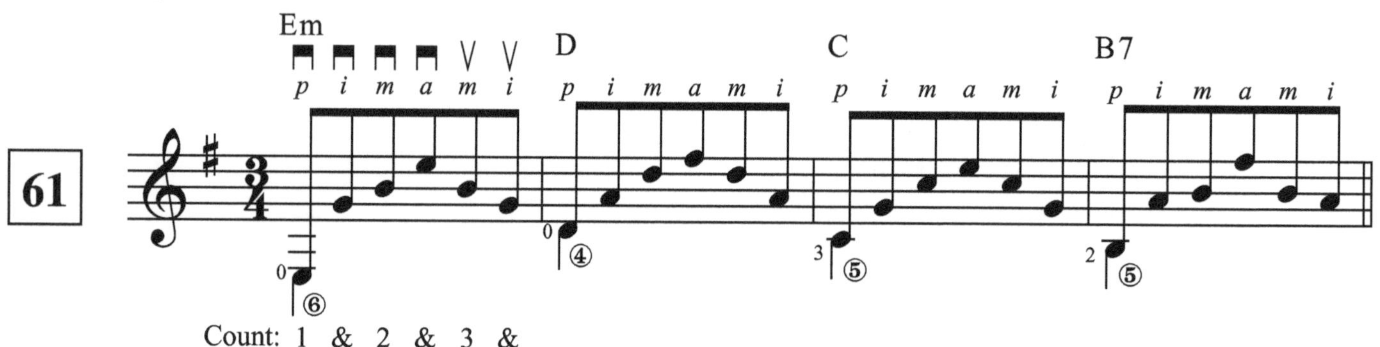

Greensleeves
(What Child Is This)

English

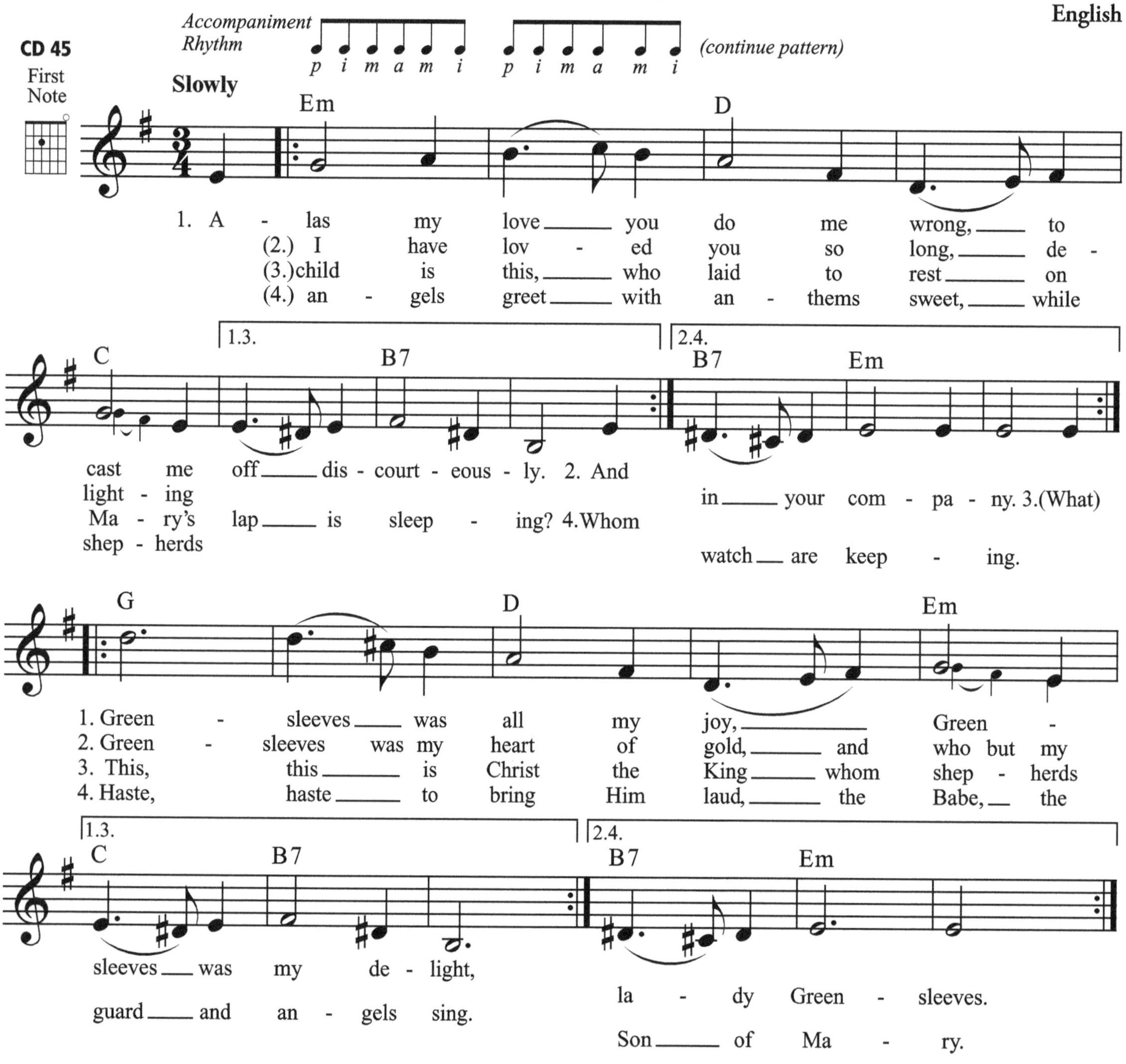

CD 45
First Note
Accompaniment Rhythm
p i m a m i
p i m a m i
(continue pattern)
Slowly
Em D
1. A - las my love you do me wrong, to
(2.) I have lov - ed you so long, de -
(3.) child is this, who laid to rest on
(4.) an - gels greet with an - thems sweet, while
C 1.3. B7 2.4. B7 Em
cast me off dis - court - eous - ly. 2. And
light - ing
Ma - ry's lap is sleep - ing? 4. Whom
shep - herds
in your com - pa - ny. 3.(What)
watch are keep - ing.
G D Em
1. Green - sleeves was all my joy, Green -
2. Green - sleeves was my heart of gold, and who but my
3. This, this is Christ the King whom shep - herds
4. Haste, haste to bring Him laud, the Babe, the
1.3. C B7 2.4. B7 Em
sleeves was my de - light,
guard and an - gels sing.
la - dy Green - sleeves.
Son of Ma - ry.

Broken Chord / Arpeggio $\frac{4}{4}$

In pickstyle, use alternating down-strokes and up-strokes with a pick, or use the sweep pick (two consecutive down-strokes) going from the 3rd to the 2nd string on **&** 2. In fingerstyle, the thumb (*p*) plucks the root of the chord, the index finger (*i*) plucks the 3rd string, the middle finger (*m*) plucks the 2nd string, and the ring finger (*a*) plucks the 1st string.

62
Em
B7
p i m i a i m i
p i m i a i m i
R
R
Count: 1 & 2 & 3 & 4 &

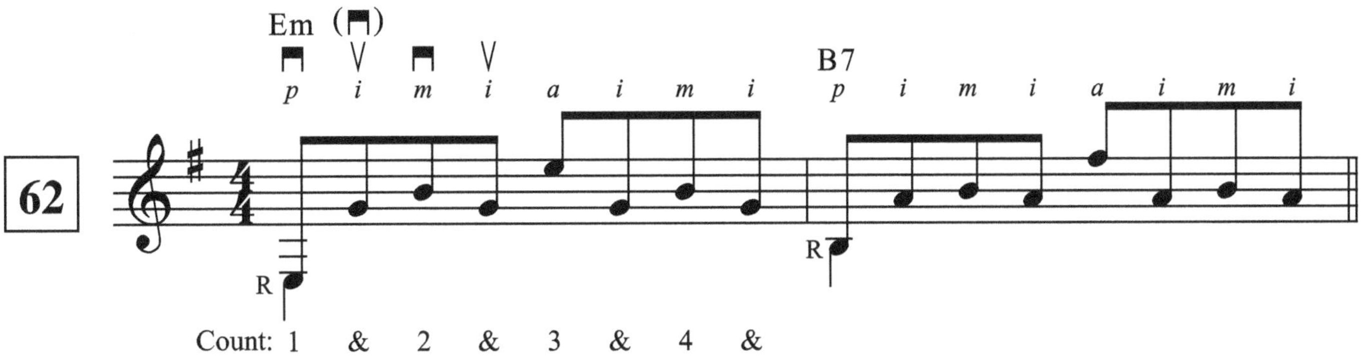

Joshua Fit the Battle of Jericho

Spiritual

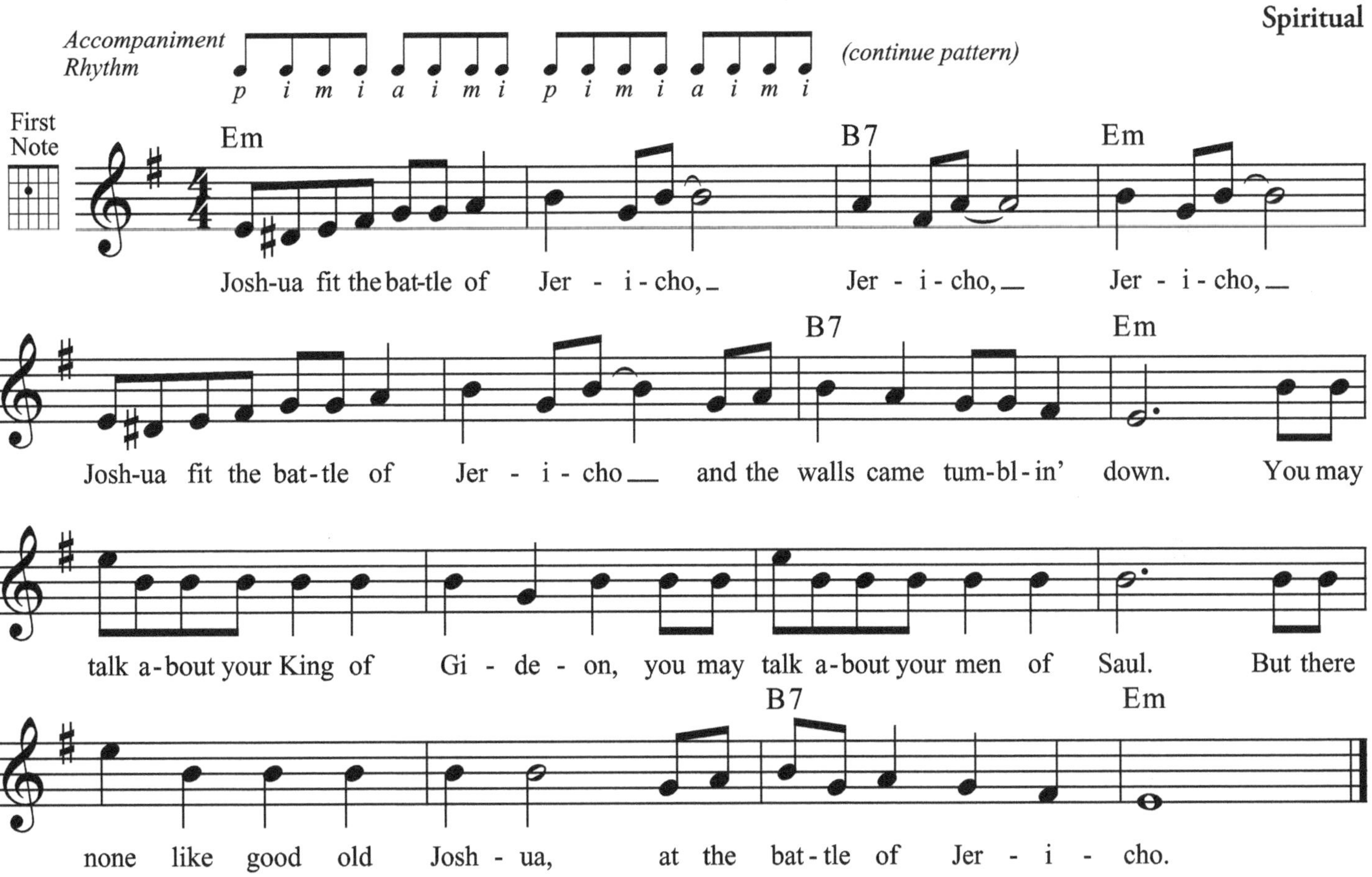

Accompaniment Rhythm
p i m i a i m i p i m i a i m i
(continue pattern)
First Note
Em
B7
Em
Josh-ua fit the bat-tle of Jer - i - cho, Jer - i - cho, Jer - i - cho,
B7
Em
Josh-ua fit the bat-tle of Jer - i - cho and the walls came tum-bl - in' down. You may
talk a-bout your King of Gi - de - on, you may talk a-bout your men of Saul. But there
B7
Em
none like good old Josh - ua, at the bat - tle of Jer - i - cho.

CD 46

Cruel War

Traditional

First Note
Slowly
G
Em
Am
1. The cruel war is rag - ing, John - ny has to
2. To - mor - row is Sun - day, Mon - day is the
B7
C
Am
G
C
G
fight; I want to be with him from morn - ing 'til night.
day that your cap - tain will call you, and you must o - bey.

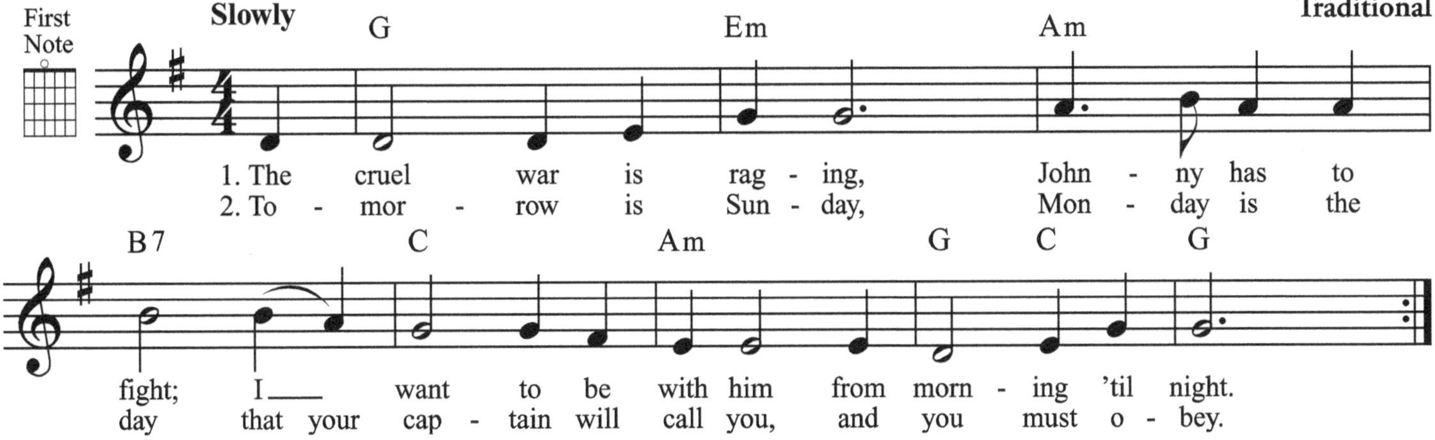

Pinch Technique

When one finger plucks simultaneously with the pick or thumb, it is called a *pinch technique.* In pickstyle, it is also referred to as a *hybrid style* because it uses both the pick and the fingers. Use a down-stroke with a pick to pluck the bass notes, and either the middle finger *(m)* or ring finger (*a*) to pluck the treble strings. On beats 3 and 4 of example 63, the middle or ring finger plucks the 1st string in combination with a down-stroke of the pick. In fingerstyle, the ring finger (*a*) pinches in combination with the thumb (*p*) on beats 3 and 4.

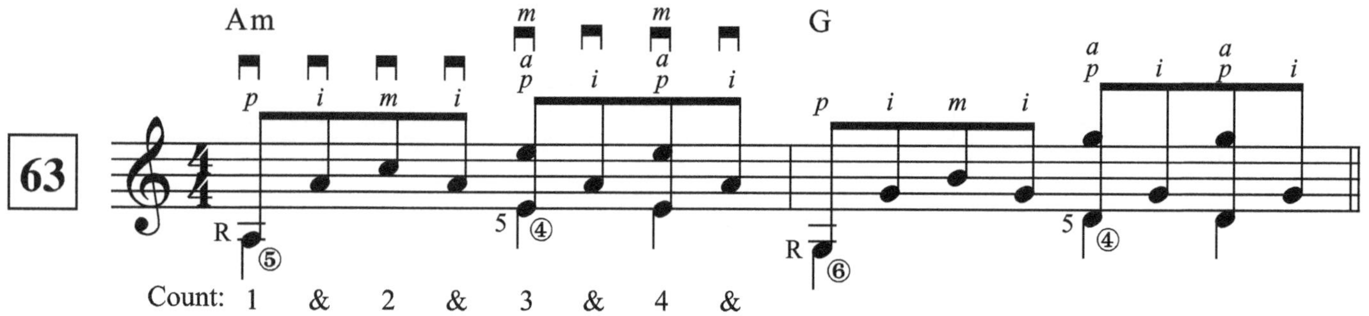

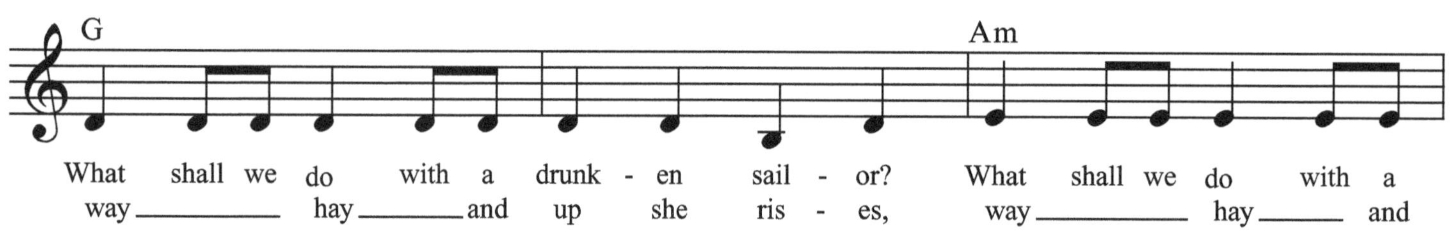

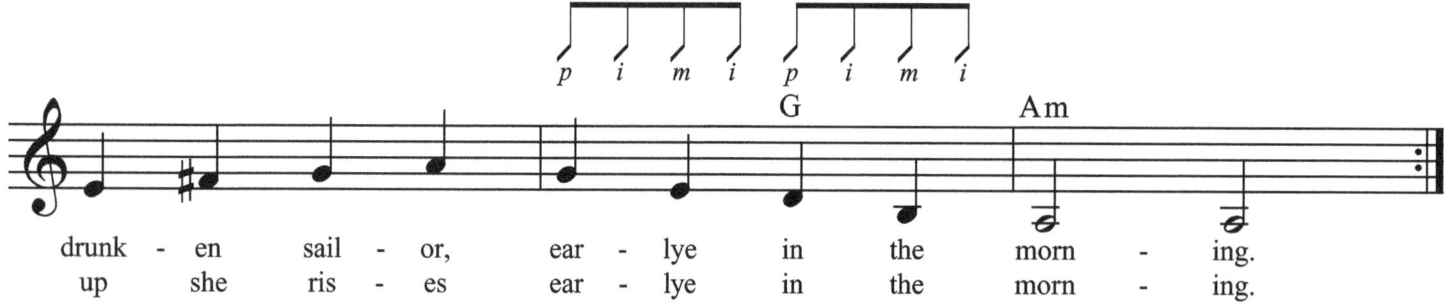

The following are additional pinch patterns that may be applied to familiar songs.

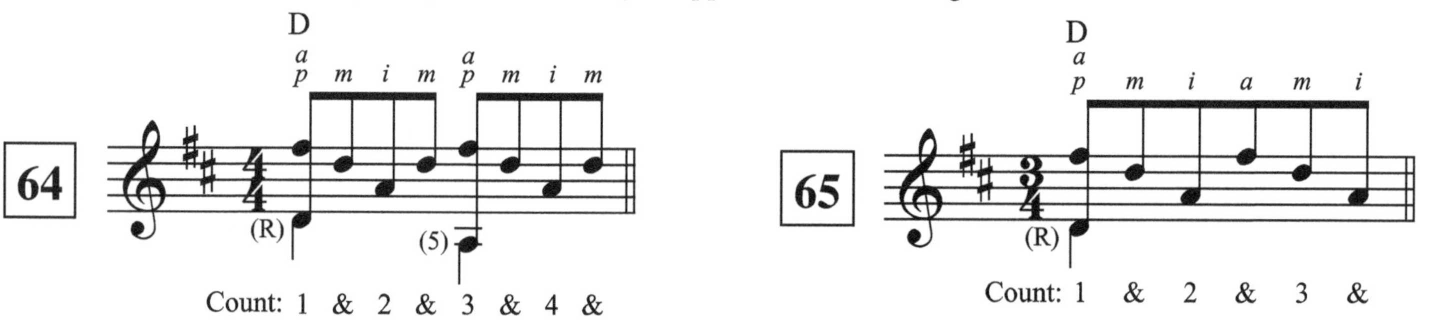

Calypso Arpeggio

To play the *calypso arpeggio* in pickstyle, use a sweep on the first four notes (consecutive down-strokes), and then alternate the pick on beats **& 4 &**. Accent (>), or give emphasis to, the 1st string. In fingerstyle, use the basic classical guitar hand position. Plant the thumb and fingers on the strings so that the thumb (*p*) plucks the root (R) of the chord, and the fingers (*i m a)* pluck the 3rd, 2nd, and 1st strings. Use free strokes.

66

Sloop John B.

Traditional

CD 48 First Note

Accompaniment Rhythm: *p i m a m i m p i m a m i m* *(continue rhythm)*

Moderate

E

So hoist up the John B. Sails, see how the main - s'ls sets.

Send for the cap - tain a - shore, let me go

B7

home.

Let me go

E

home,

E7

let me go

A

home.

Am

I

E

feel so break - up,

B7

I want to go

E

home.

In the following variation, accents are very important. It will help to think of the rhythm pattern as **1** 2 3 **1** 2 3 **1** 2.

67

FINGER-PICKING

Finger-picking is an instrumental style of playing guitar that was developed by black Southern American musicians around 1900. Early innovators of this style include Mississippi John Hurt, Blind Blake, Robert Johnson, Mance Lipscomb, and Rev. Gary Davis. This style is reminiscent of the piano swing-bass and ragtime styles of playing, and it is primarily performed with the thumb and fingers. On the guitar, the picking hand thumb plays a rhythmic bass on every downbeat while the fingers pick out the melody on the treble strings. This produces a sound similar to the pianist playing a "boom-chuck" pattern with the left hand while the right hand plays the melody.

One of the most notable and influential finger-picking guitarists was Merle Travis. Travis developed a fingerstyle picking technique for guitar that became so identified with him that it bears his name: "Travis picking." "Country pickin'," "three finger pickin'," and just plain "pickin'" are various names given to this guitar style. The two most distinguishing characteristics of the Travis picking style are the **steady beat** established by the thumb or pick playing on every downbeat (**1**&**2**&**3**&**4**&), and the **syncopated** patterns produced by the fingers plucking the treble strings on the upbeats (1**&**2**&**3**&**4**&**).

Pickstyle

As the name suggests, finger-picking is essentially a fingerstyle technique. Pickstyle players, however, can assimilate the style by using a combination of pick and fingerstyle technique referred to as the *hybrid* style. The pick is used to pluck the bass patterns, and the middle and ring fingers are used to pluck the treble strings.

Fingerstyle

The thumb plays on every downbeat. To achieve the necessary speed and avoid interference with the fingers, use a free stroke with the thumb (see page 12). In the free stroke, the thumb does not come to rest on the adjacent higher-pitched string. Also use free strokes with the index and middle fingers (see page 51).

Playing Position

1. Place the forearm on the edge of the guitar above the bridge base.
2. The index finger (*i*) is placed on the 2nd string (B).
3. The middle finger (*m*) is placed on the 1st string (E).
4. Keep the thumb rigid, straight, and extended.

Finger-picking hand position.

Fingerstyle. The thumb (*p*) plucks on every downbeat. Play the root of the D chord on beats 1 and 3, and the 3rd string on beats 2 and 4 (Ex. 68). In Ex. 69 and 70, the index finger (*i*) and middle finger (*m*) are added to the pattern. It is important to accent certain tones plucked with the fingers.

Pickstyle. While holding the D chord, begin to "groove" the pick pattern (Ex. 68). The pick plucks on every downbeat and alternates between the root of the chord and the 3rd string. In Ex. 69, the middle finger (*m*) plucks the 2nd string, and in Ex. 70, the ring finger (*a*) is used to pluck the 1st string.

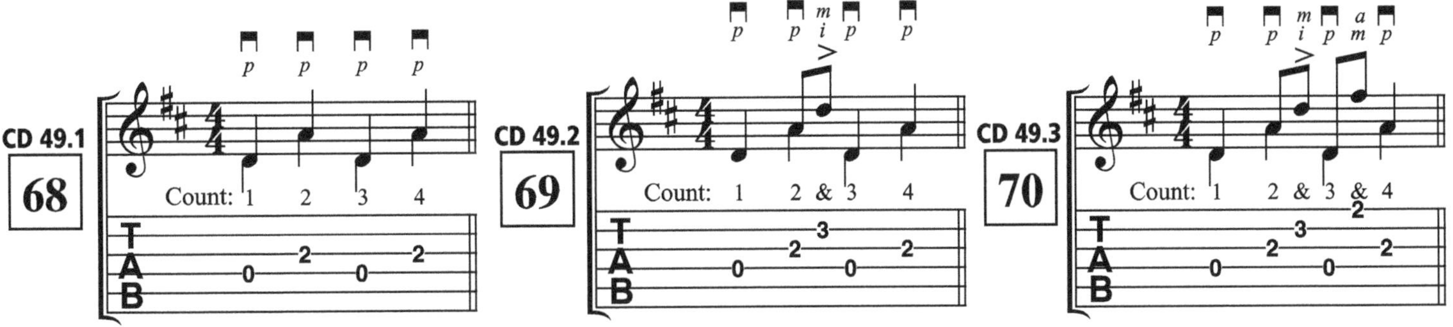

Apply the finger-picking pattern introduced in example 70 to "Reuben's Train."

Reuben's Train

In "Little Maggie," the pick and thumb patterns remain the same on all chords: root–3rd string–root–3rd string. On the C and A7 chords, the thumb or pick alternates between the 5th string (R) and the 3rd string.

Alternate Bass

In the *alternate bass* pattern, the thumb or pick plucks the fifth (5) of the chord on beat 3 of the measure. Continue to pluck the 3rd string on beats 2 and 4. This pattern remains the same regardless of the chord.

Other Patterns

The thumb or pick continues the same pattern but the finger pattern is changed in the following finger-picking patterns. Alternating to the fifth (5) of the chord is optional.

Pinch Patterns

In *fingerstyle*, when the thumb and index finger, or thumb and middle finger, pluck the bass and treble strings together, it is called a *pinch* technique. In *pickstyle*, the pick and the middle or ring finger pluck the bass and treble strings together, called a *hybrid* technique.

CD 54.1

78

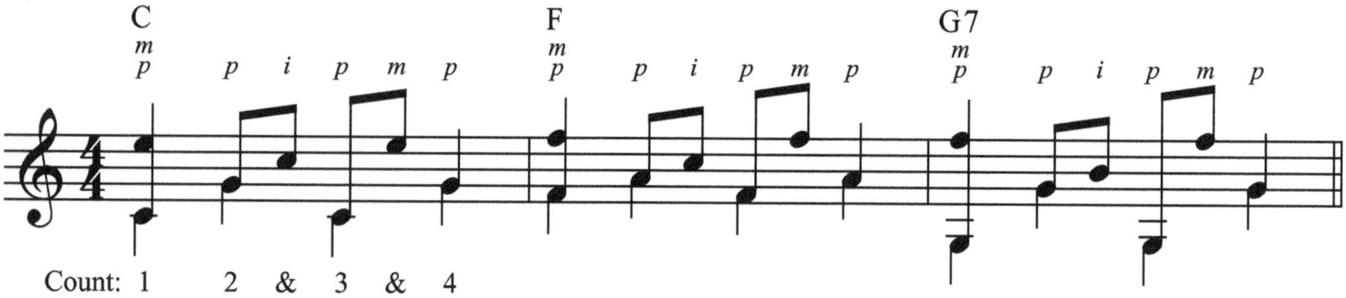

C
m
p p i p m p
F
m
p p i p m p
G7
m
p p i p m p
Count: 1 2 & 3 & 4

Railroad Bill

Traditional

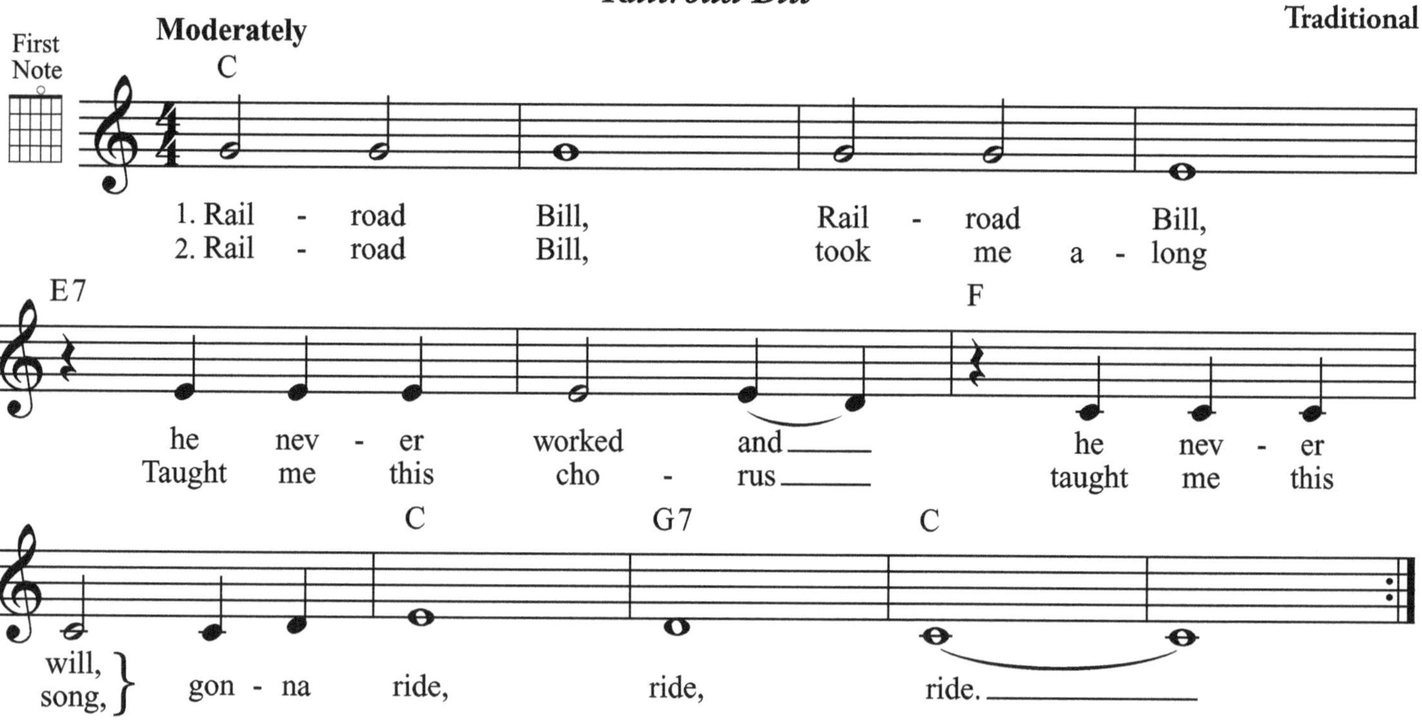

First Note
Moderately
C
1. Rail - road Bill, Rail - road Bill,
2. Rail - road Bill, took me a - long
E7
he nev - er worked and
Taught me this cho - rus
F
he nev - er
taught me this
C G7 C
will, song, gon - na ride, ride, ride.

Try applying the following pinch patterns to songs you know. Alternate the thumb or pick to the fifth (5) on beat 3 of the measure when you have the patterns "grooved."

CD 54.2

79

C
p
m
p
p i p
Count: 1 2 3 & 4

CD 54.3

80

C
m
p
p i
m
p
i p
Count: 1 2 & 3 & 4

CD 54.4

81

C
m
p
m
p
p i p
Count: 1 2 3 & 4

CD 54.5

82

C
p m p i
m
p
p
Count: 1 & 2 & 3 4

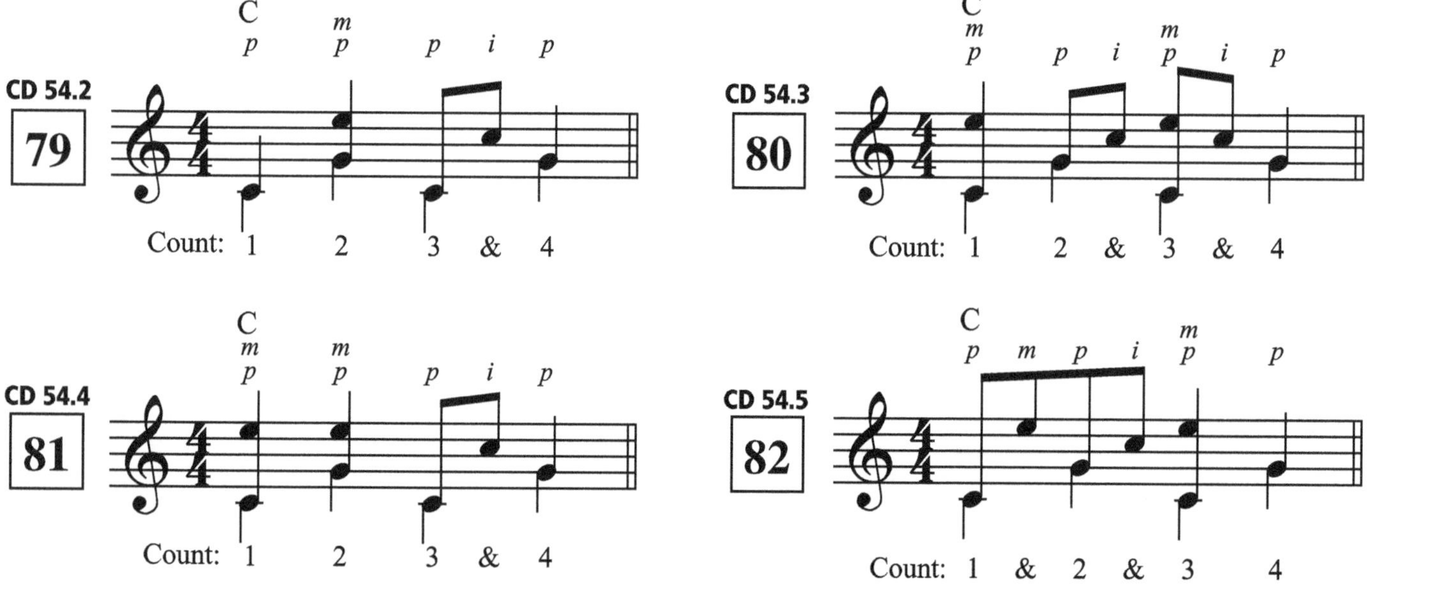

Try various finger-picking patterns with the following songs. The goal is to eventually "break out" of patterns and use more than one accompaniment rhythm. Try mixing it up a little. Develop new patterns.

Michael, Row the Boat Ashore

Traditional

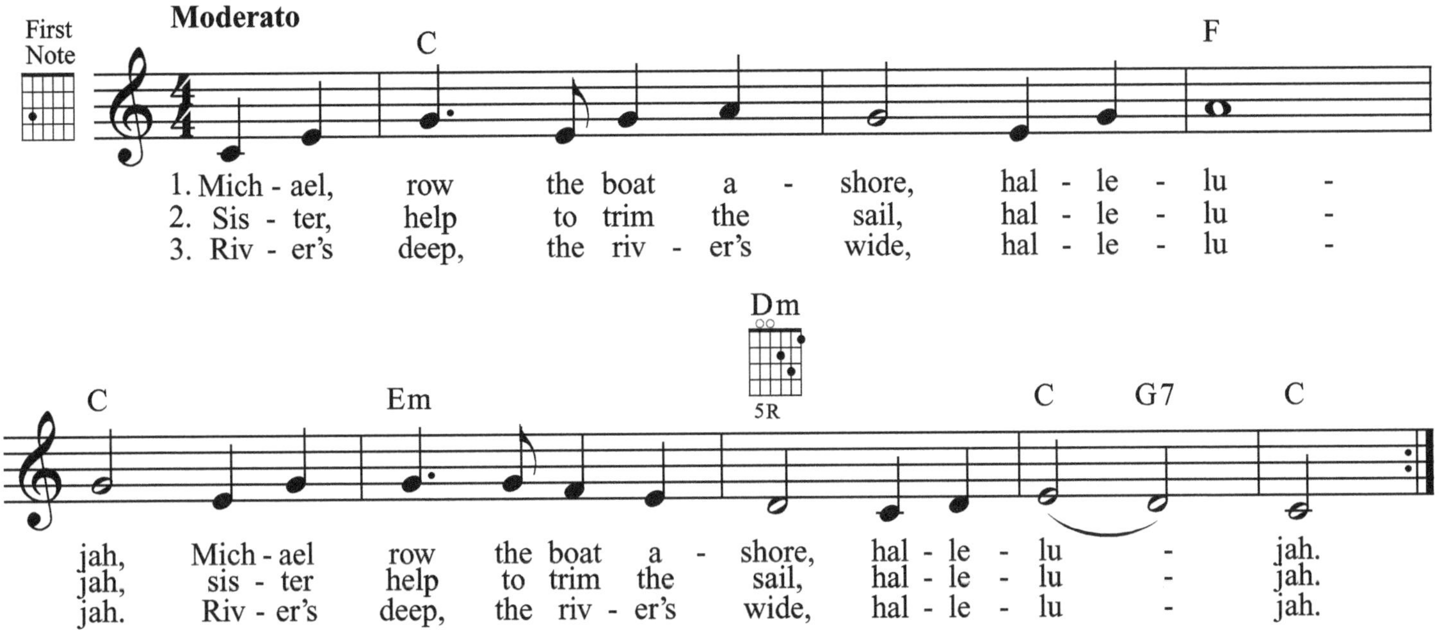

Moderato

First Note

C F

1. Mich - ael, row the boat a - shore, hal - le - lu -
2. Sis - ter, help to trim the sail, hal - le - lu -
3. Riv - er's deep, the riv - er's wide, hal - le - lu -

C Em Dm (5R) C G7 C

jah, Mich - ael row the boat a - shore, hal - le - lu - jah.
jah, sis - ter help to trim the sail, hal - le - lu - jah.
jah. Riv - er's deep, the riv - er's wide, hal - le - lu - jah.

Every Night When the Sun Goes Down

Traditional

Slowly

First Note

C G7 C Em

1. Ev - 'ry night ___ when the sun goes down, ___ ev - 'ry night ___
(2.) love don't weep ___ true love don't mourn, ___ true love don't weep ___

C7 G7 Dm G7

___ when the sun goes down. ___ Ev - 'ry night ___ when the sun goes
___ true love don't mourn. ___ True love don't weep ___ true love don't

Am Dm G7 C

down, ___ I hang my head ___ and mourn - ful cry. ___ 2. True.
mourn, ___ I goin' a - way ___ to Mar - ble - town. ___

SECTION TWO: NOTATION

Section Two includes theory, music notation, songs, and ensembles. The material in this section should be studied in conjunction with the chords and accompaniment presented in Section One. Either **pickstyle** or **fingerstyle** pick techniques may be applied in the notation section. In *pickstyle*, a pick is used to pluck the strings. In *fingerstyle*, the index finger (*i*) and middle finger (*m*) will generally pluck the treble strings with *rest strokes*, and the thumb (*p*) will pluck the bass strings with *free strokes*. In classical guitar, the free stroke is called a *tirando* and the rest stroke is called an *apoyando*.

Pickstyle

The pick (also called a flat-pick or plectrum) is held between the thumb and index finger of the picking hand. It is similar to how you hold a key when unlocking a door.

1. Bend the index finger toward the thumb.
2. Place the thumb on the side of the index finger along the first joint.
3. Insert the pick between the thumb and the index finger so that a triangle is exposed.

A variety of pick sizes and thicknesses (gauges) are available. Review page 8.

Pick position.

Down-stroke. The *down-stroke* (⊓) is the basic stroke. When stroking the strings, do not allow the thumb to collapse. Use a wrist motion and keep the thumb rigid. The thumb pushes the pick through the string, stops short of the lower-pitched string, and immediately returns to the starting position. The middle, ring, and little fingers on the picking hand can lightly touch the guitar and move with the hand. I don't recommend anchoring any portion of the right hand on the guitar. The angle of the pick should be fairly upright (see page 8).

Up-stroke. The *up-stroke* (V) is primarily used to play notes on up-beats (&), as when playing eighth notes. When playing the up-stroke, follow through only enough to finish picking the string, and then immediately return to the starting point. Use **alternating** down-strokes and up-strokes (⊓ V) to play successive eighth notes. Use an economy of motion. Stop short of the adjacent strings when picking alternating down- and up-strokes.

Fingerstyle

Rest strokes (index and middle fingers). Perform the *rest stroke* by plucking (pressing, or pushing) the string and coming to rest on the next lower-pitched string. The **primary** motion for the rest stroke comes from the third finger joint, where the finger joins the hand. Do not allow the fingers to collapse at the first joint. **Alternate** the index finger (*i*) and middle finger (*m*) when playing successive single notes or melodies.

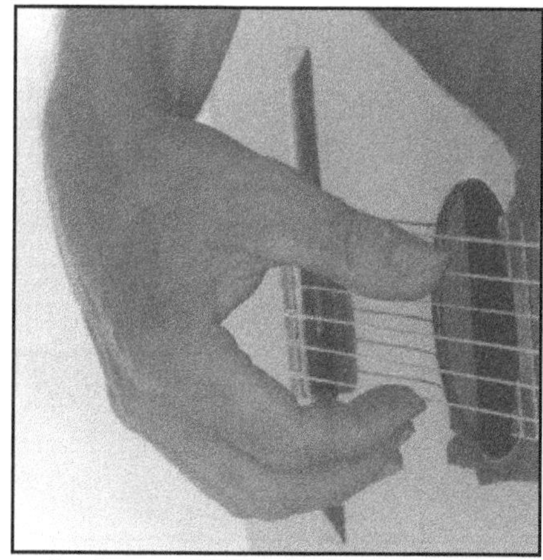

Index finger, preparation.

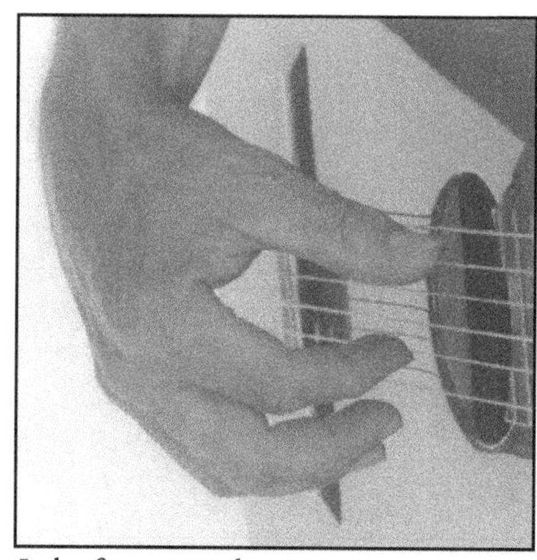

Index finger, completion.

Rest strokes with the index and middle fingers are used to play single-note lead lines and melodies. Learn to *alternate* the index finger (*i*) and middle finger (*m*). In general, when you are working out alternating patterns (*i m* or *m i*), try to use the middle finger when moving to higher-sounding strings and the index finger when moving to lower-sounding strings. The index and middle fingers can be used to play rest strokes on the treble strings as well as the bass strings. On the open 1st string (E), practice playing whole notes with the index and middle fingers.

	i	*m*	*i*	*m*
Count:	1 - 2 - 3 - 4	1 - 2 - 3 - 4	1 - 2 - 3 - 4	1 - 2 - 3 - 4

Free and rest strokes (thumb). I recommend using a *free stroke* with the thumb when playing the bass notes in the notation section (review page 12). However, a *rest stroke* with the thumb can be used to give more power to a particular tone. With the forearm resting on the edge of the guitar, above the bridge base, pluck the 4th string with the thumb and let it come to rest on the 3rd string. The 3rd string is used to "brake" the thumb's downward motion. Keep the thumb rigid. The motion of the rest stroke comes from the joint where the thumb joins the hand. Do not bend the thumb at the first joint.

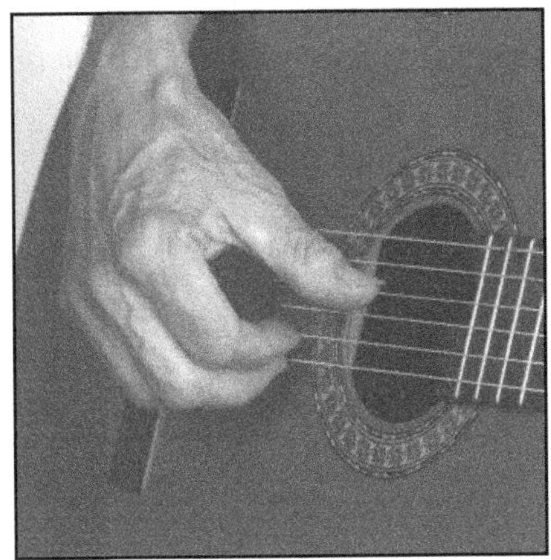

Thumb, preparation.

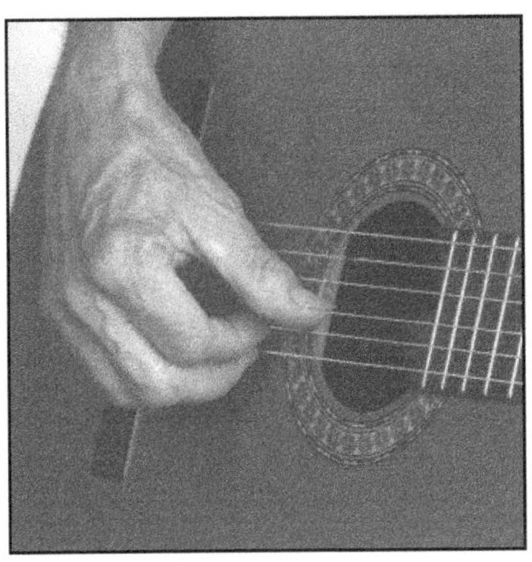

Thumb, completion.

Explanation of Symbols

In fingerstyle notation, *p, i, m,* and *a* placed above notes indicate the picking-hand fingers to use to pluck them.

p = thumb (*pulgar*)
i = index finger (*indice*)
m = middle finger (*medio*)
a = ring finger (*anular*)

Circled numbers ⑥⑤④③②① placed below notes indicate which strings to play.

The numbers 1, 2, 3, and 4 placed next to notes indicate the fingers of the fretting hand. A zero (0) stands for an open string.

In pickstyle notation, ⊓ indicates a *down-stroke,* and V indicates an *up-stroke.*

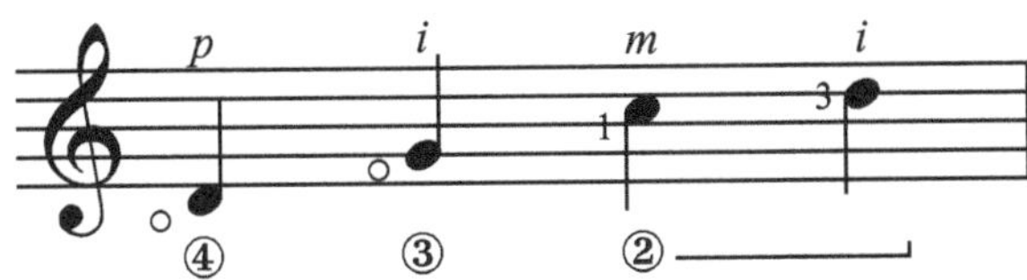

Notes are placed on the *staff,* which consists of five lines and four spaces. The first seven letters of the alphabet are used to name the notes: A B C D E F G.

The *treble clef,* or *G clef,* placed on the staff designates the second line as the note G.

Note: Guitar notation **sounds** an octave (eight notes) lower than **written.**

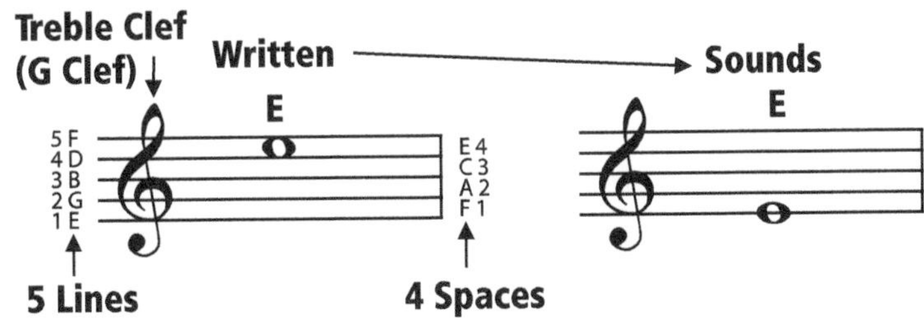

NOTES ON THE 3RD STRING

G: OPEN, 3RD STRING

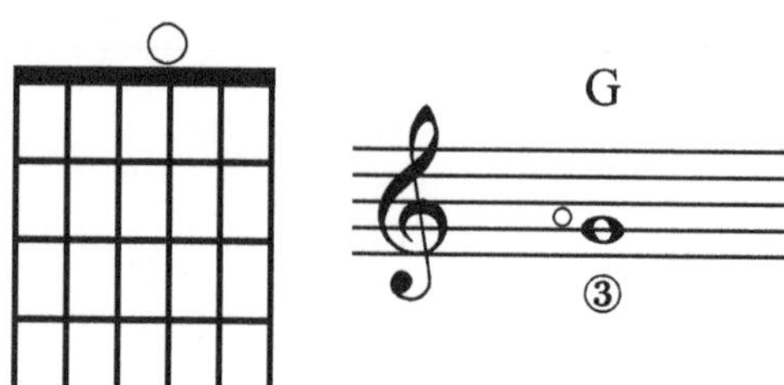

The open 3rd string is the note G. It is located on the second line of the music staff.

Whole Note

In most music, a *whole note* receives four *beats*, or *counts*.

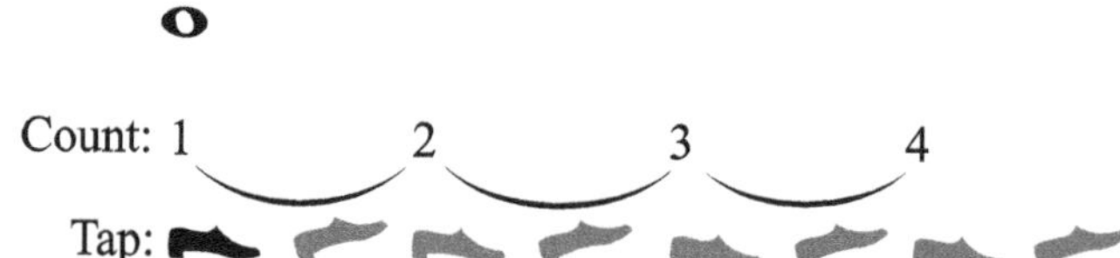

Play example 1 using either pickstyle or fingerstyle techniques. In pickstyle, use a down-stroke on each note. In fingerstyle, alternate the index finger (*i*) and middle finger (*m*) using a *rest stroke*, also called an *apoyando*. The chord symbols above the notation are for teacher accompaniment.

CD 55.1

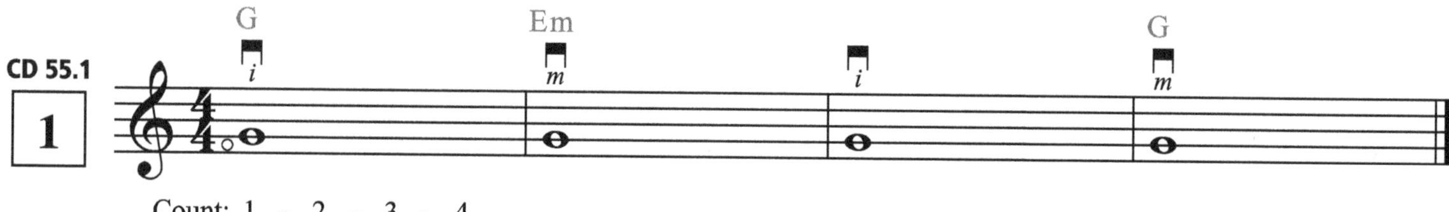

Half Note

The *half note* receives two beats. It has only half as much time value as the whole note.

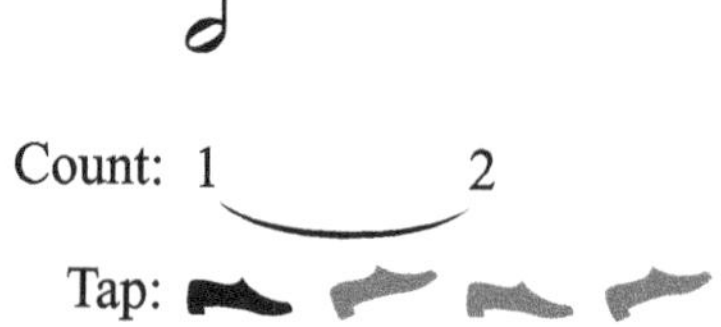

CD 55.2

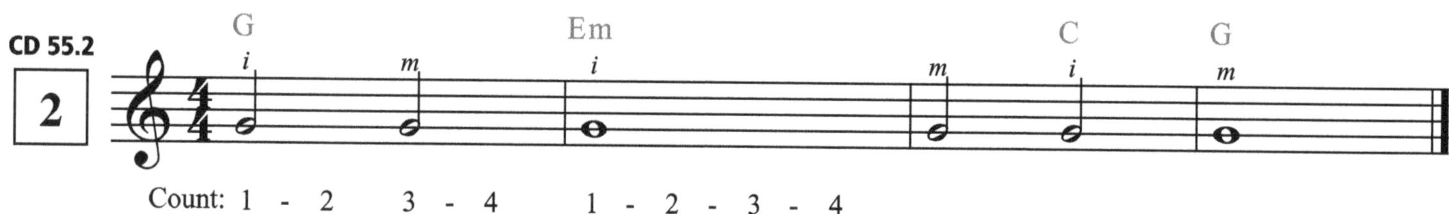

A: 2ND FRET, 3RD STRING

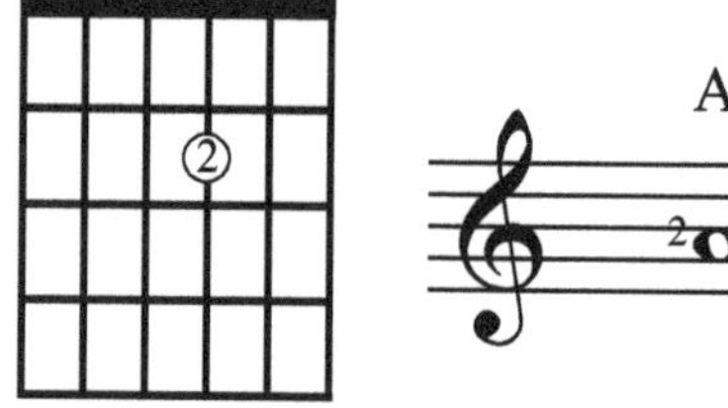

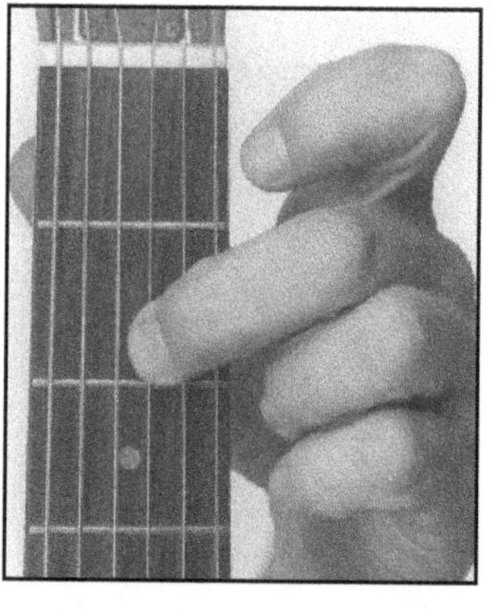

Place the 2nd finger of the fretting hand on the 2nd fret, 3rd string, Apply the pressure close to the fret to avoid "buzz." In music notation, the A is located on the second space of the music staff.

Now combine the G and A.

Quarter Note

In most music, the quarter note receives one beat.

NOTES ON THE 2ND STRING

B: OPEN, 2ND STRING

The open 2nd string is tuned to B. In music notation, the B is located on the third line of the music staff.

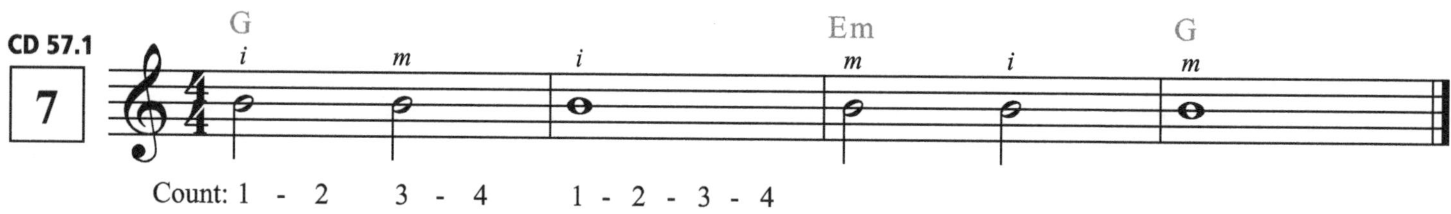

Review the notes G, A, and B. Circled numbers indicate strings.

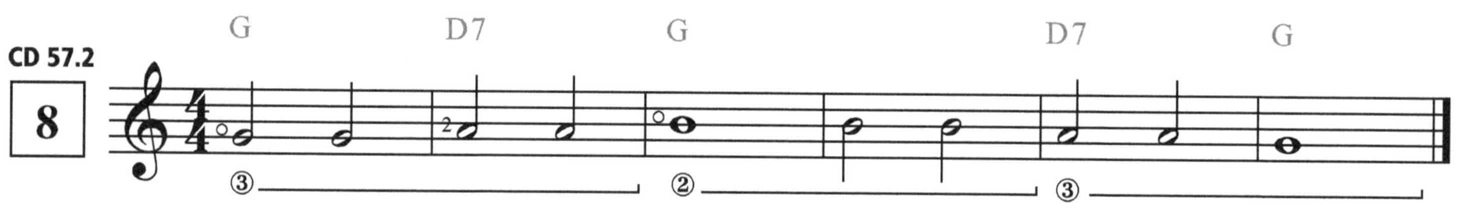

At Pierrot's Door

Traditional

C: 1ST FRET, 2ND STRING

①

C
1
②

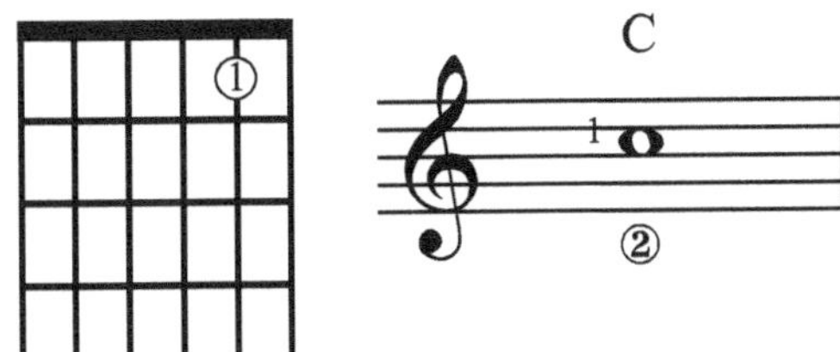

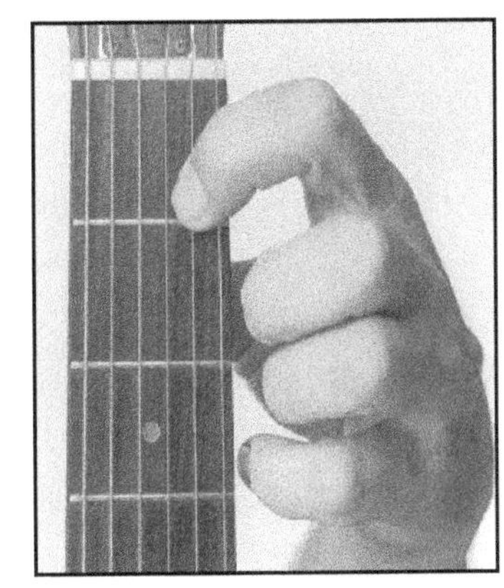

Place the 1st finger of the fretting hand on the 1st fret, 2nd string. Fingernails need to be short.

CD 59.1

11

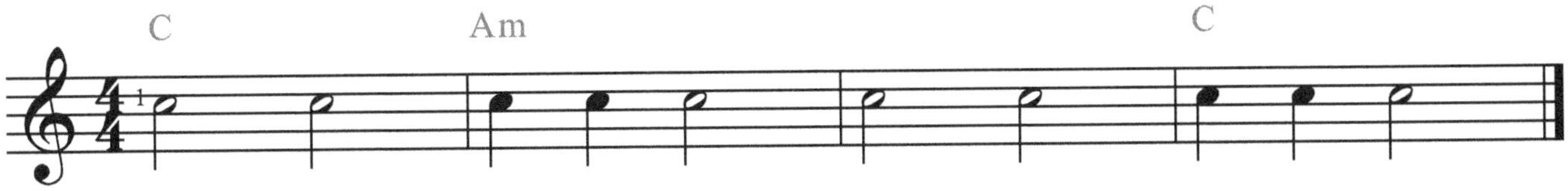

C
Am
C

CD 59.2

12

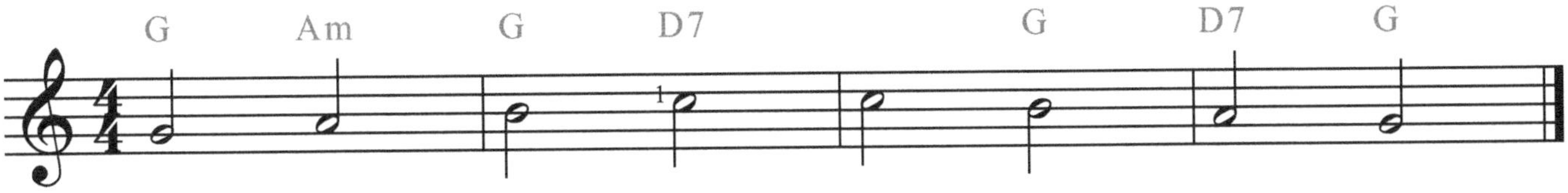

G
Am
G
D7
G
D7
G

Nancy

Slowly

CD 59.3

13

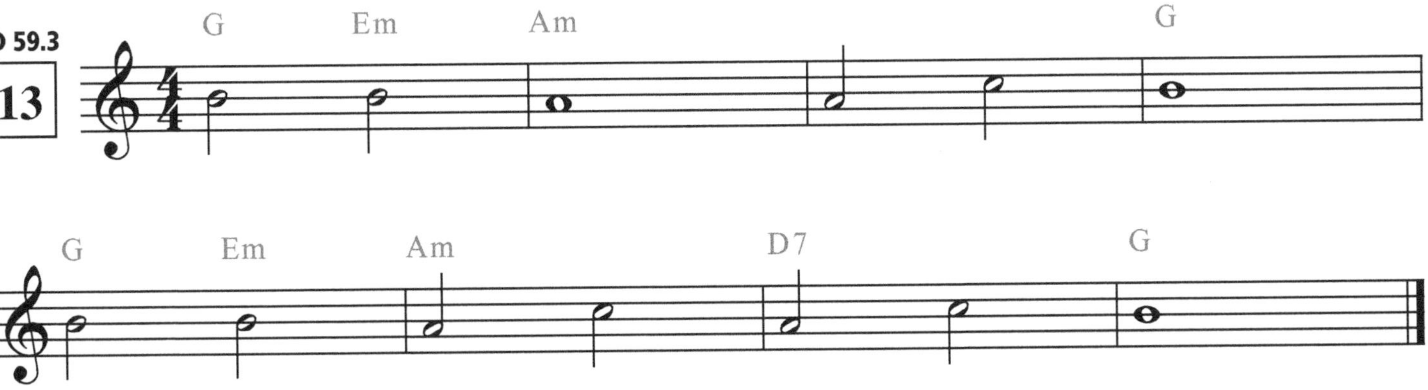

G
Em
Am
G
G
Em
Am
D7
G

ENSEMBLE

CD 60

14

First Duet

G
Em
Am
D7
G
Gtr. I
Gtr. II

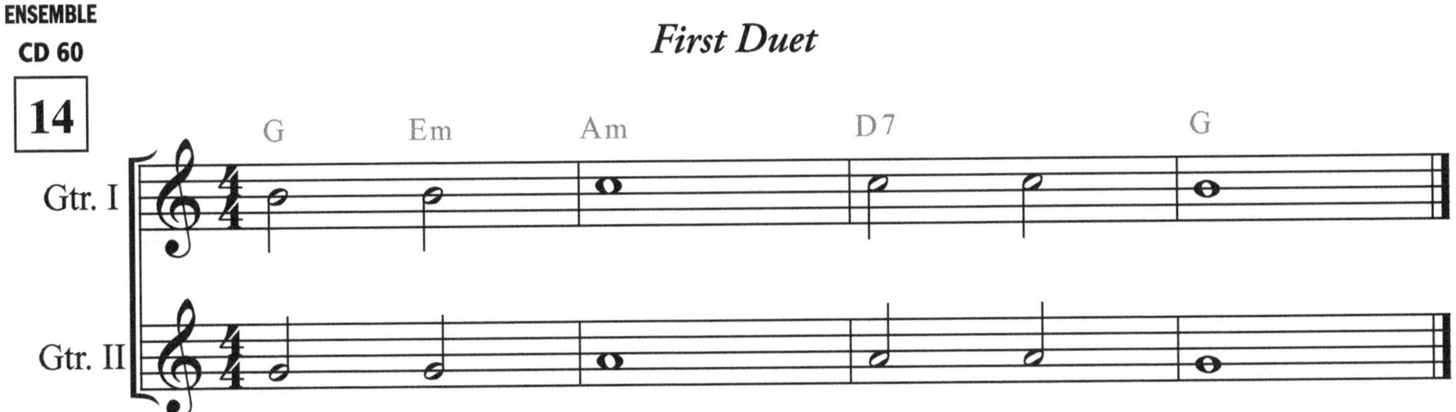

Optional: Add a chord accompaniment to "First Duet."

Dotted Half Note

A dot may be added to any note. The dot adds one-half the note's time value. A *dotted half note* gets three beats.

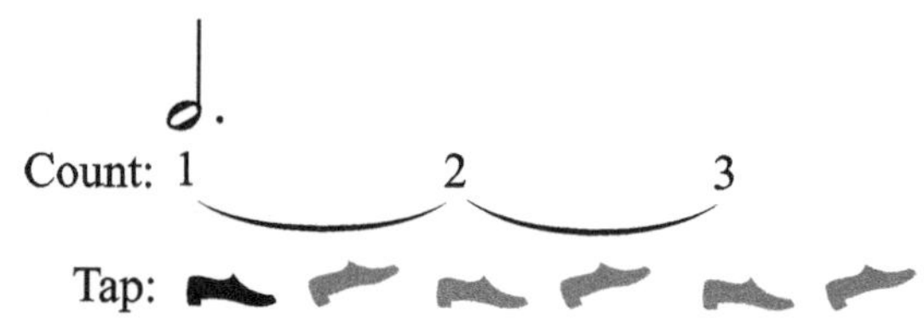

$\frac{3}{4}$ Time Signature

Beats are grouped together to form *measures*. Measures are divided by *bar lines*. The *time signature* tells how many beats are in each measure.

3 = 3 beats in each measure
4 = quarter note gets one beat

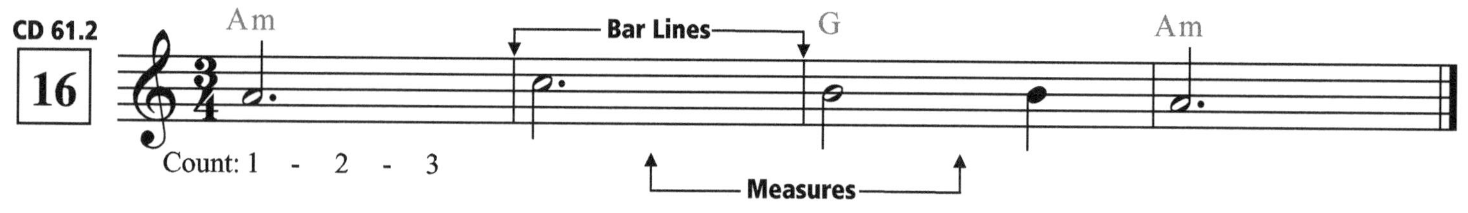

Wendy's Mood

D: 3RD FRET, 2ND STRING

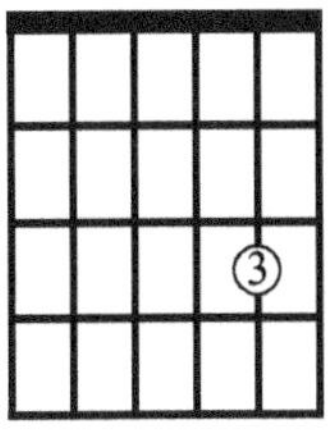

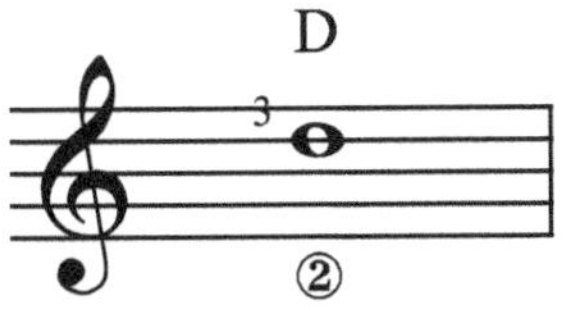
D

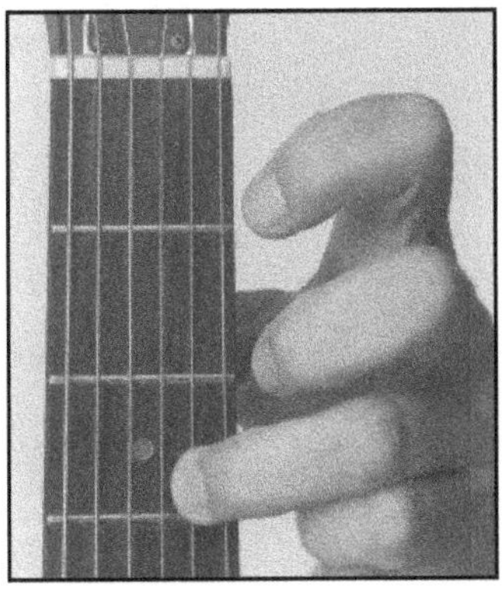

Place the 3rd finger on the 3rd fret, 2nd string. The palm of your hand should not touch the neck of the guitar. Keep the 1st and 2nd fingers over the fretboard.

CD 63.1

18

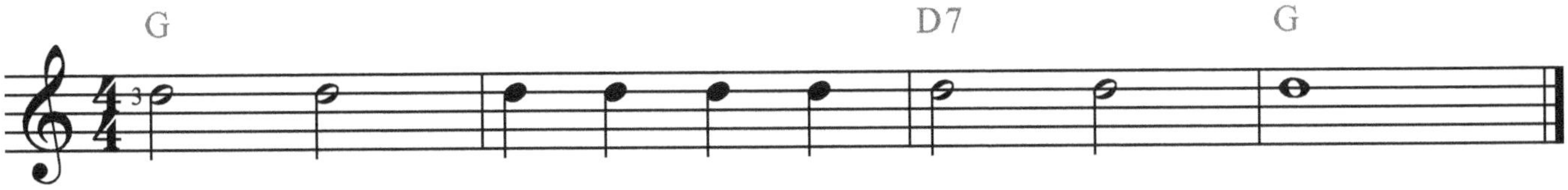
G
D7
G

CD 63.2

19

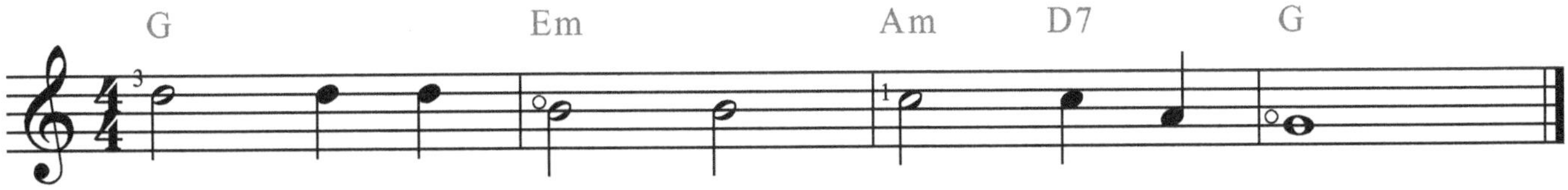
G
Em
Am
D7
G

Jesu, Joy of Man's Desiring
(melody)

J.S. Bach

ENSEMBLE
CD 64

20

Slowly

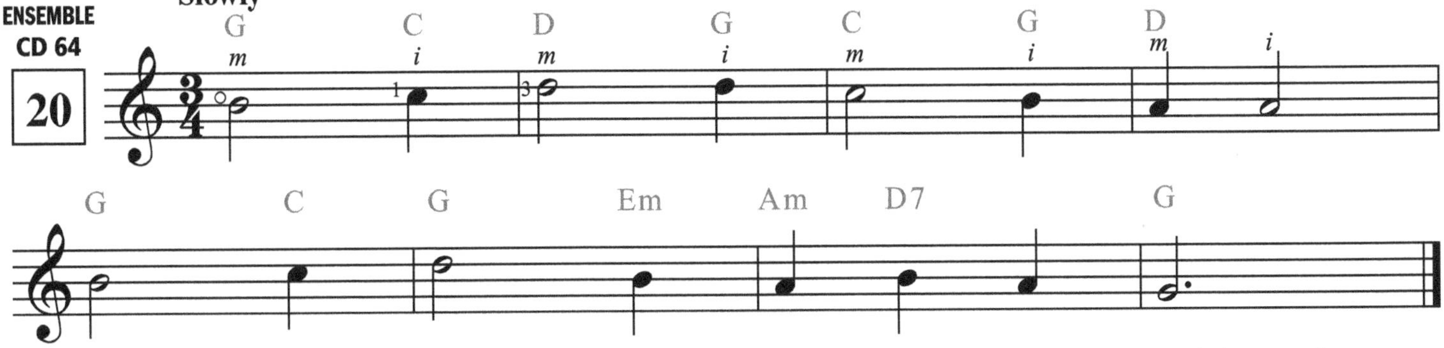
G
C
D
G
C
G
D
G
C
G
Em
Am
D7
G

"Jesu, Joy of Man's Desiring," example 20, may be combined with example 77 on page 90 (bass and alto parts).

ENSEMBLE
CD 65

21

Lightly Row
(duet)

Traditional

Moderate

G
D7
G
Gtr. I
Gtr. II
D7
G
D7
G

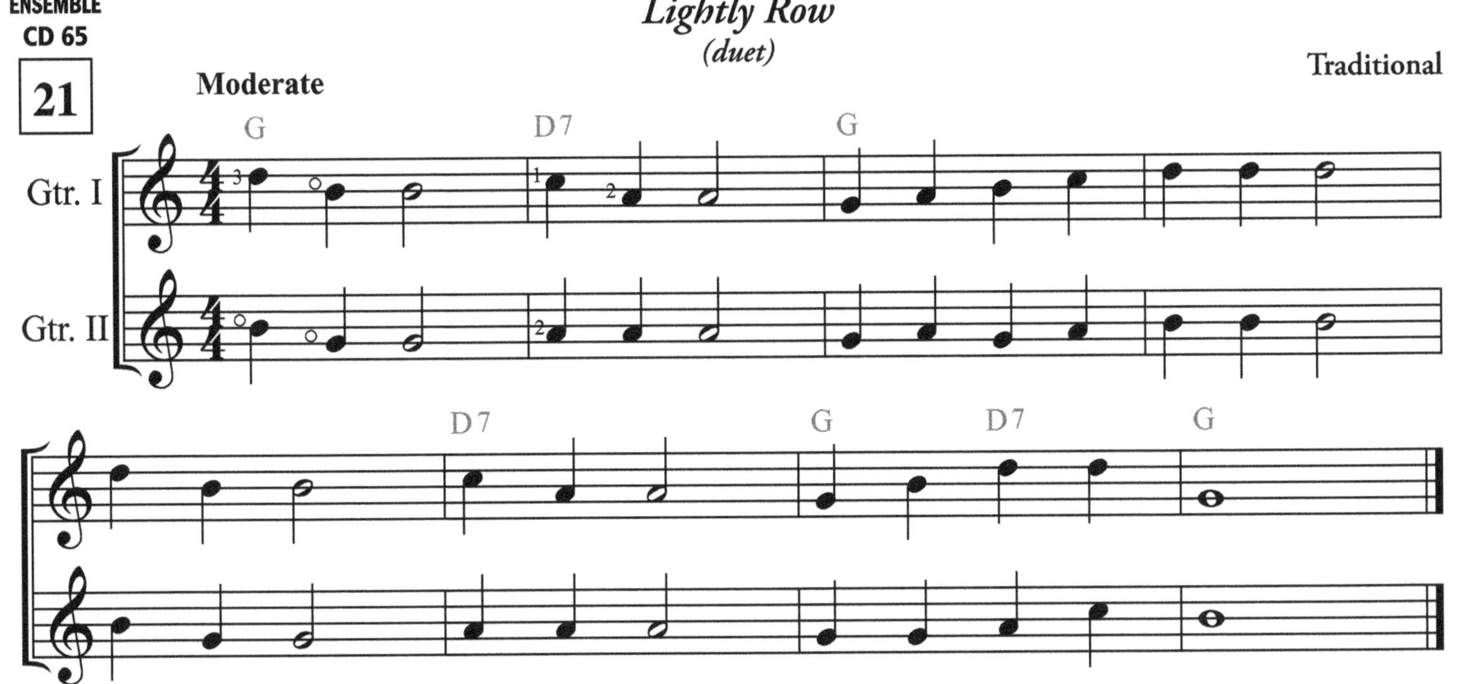

Eighth Notes

An *eighth note* receive one half of a beat and can be played on the **down** or the **up** part of the beat. Two eighth notes equal one quarter note.

In pickstyle, use down-strokes (⊓) on downbeats, and up-strokes (V) on upbeats.

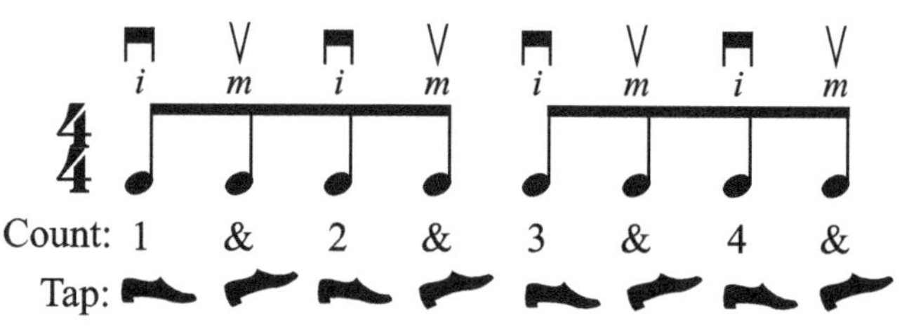

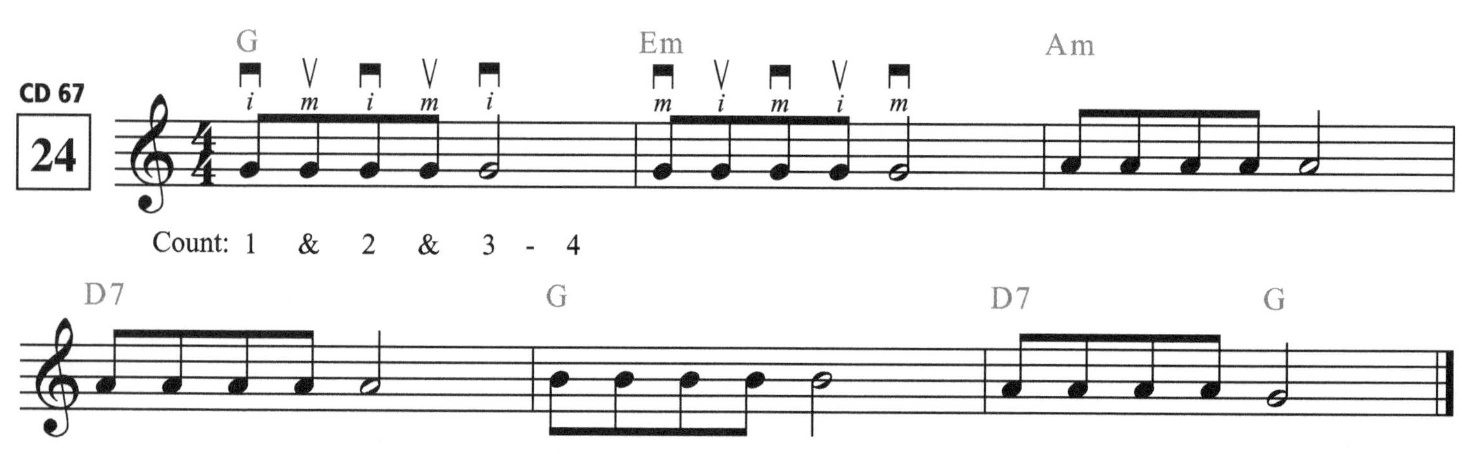

$\frac{2}{4}$ Time Signature

In music with a $\frac{2}{4}$ time signature, the beats are in groups of two, and there are two beats in each measure. The first beat of each measure should receive slightly more stress, or weight.

2 = 2 beats in each measure
4 = quarter note gets one beat

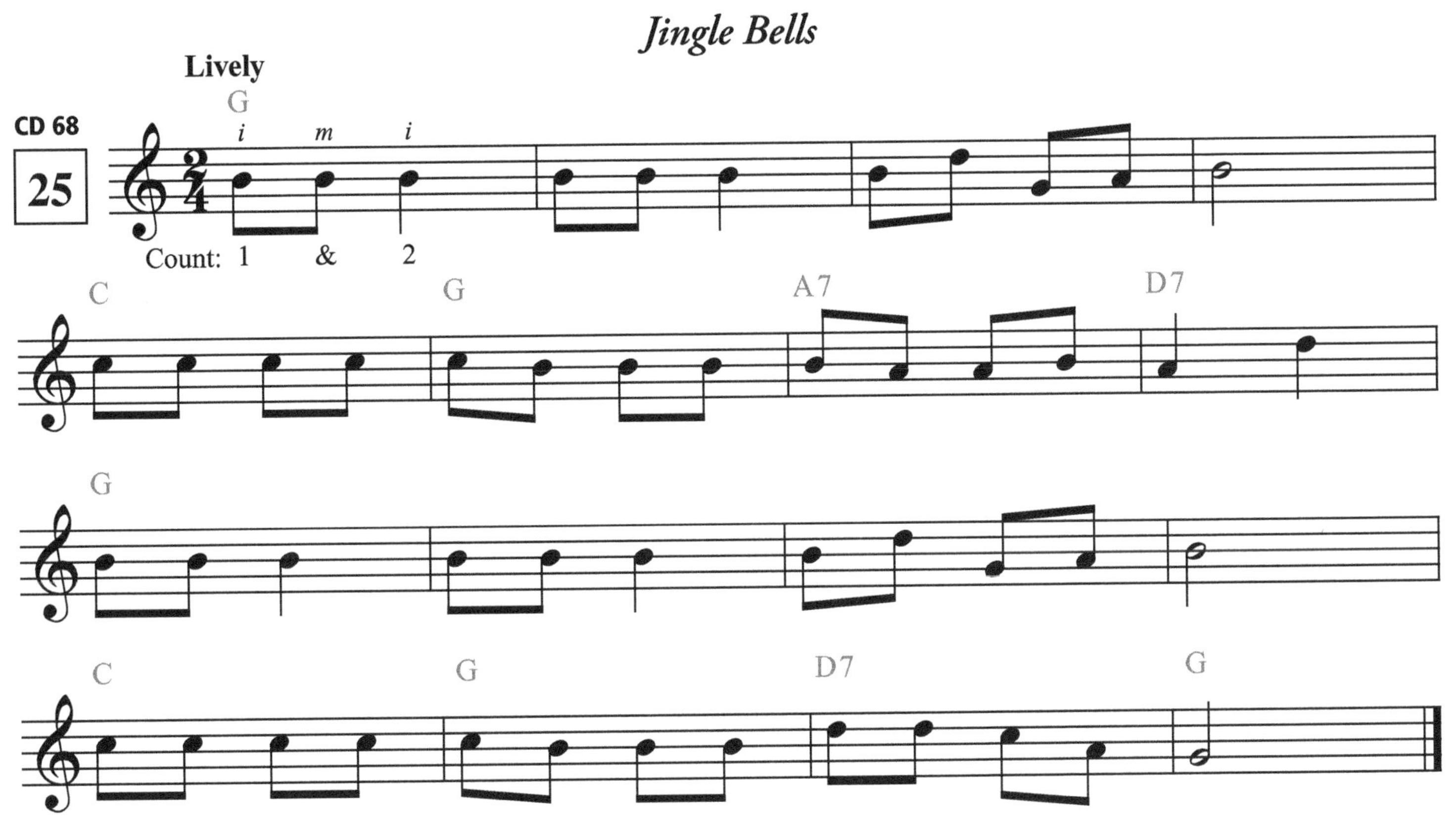

Repeat Signs

Repeat signs are used in notation to avoid writing out repeated passages of music. Repeat signs consist of two dots placed before or after a *double bar,* facing the music that is to be repeated. Repeat the music enclosed within the signs.

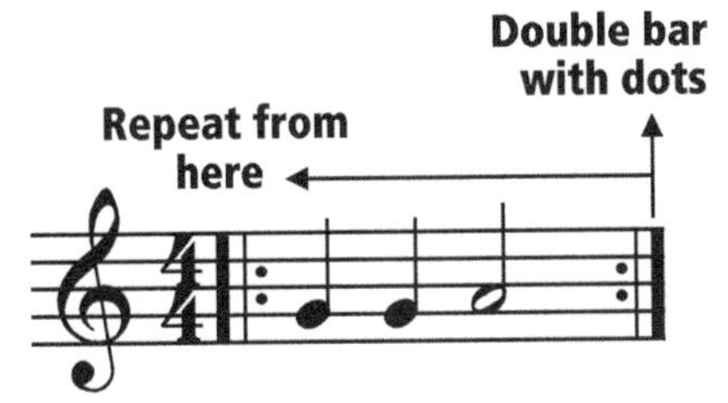

"Little Bird," example 26, may be combined with example 56 on page 84 (bass part).

NOTES ON THE 1ST STRING

E: OPEN, 1ST STRING

The open 1st string is tuned to E. In music notation, the E is located on the fourth space of the music staff.

Ned's Blues
(melody)

"Ned's Blues," example 31, can be combined with example 48 on page 81.

Dotted Quarter Note

A dot added to a quarter note adds one-half beat. The *dotted quarter note* receives one and one-half beats. Most often, the dotted quarter note is followed by an eighth note. This rhythm pattern exists in the beginning of two familiar songs: "London Bridge" and "Deck the Halls."

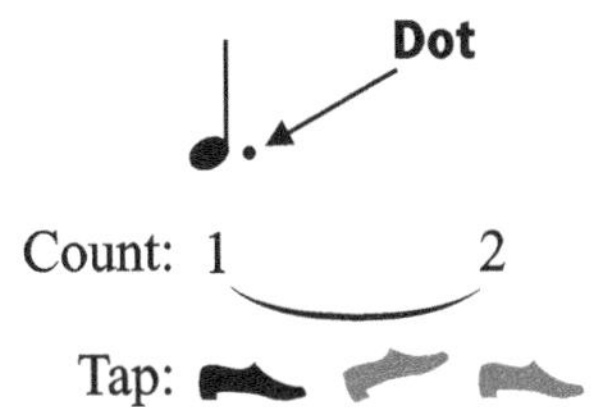

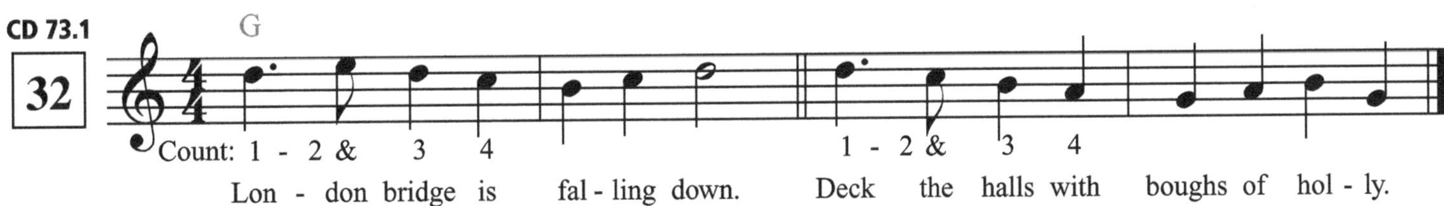

Michael, Row the Boat Ashore

Traditional

All Through the Night

Traditional

Tie

The time value of one note may be added to another note of the same pitch with the use of the *tie*. A tie is necessary if you wish to hold a note beyond a bar line. Curved lines (⌒ or ‿) "tie" the time value of two or more notes together.

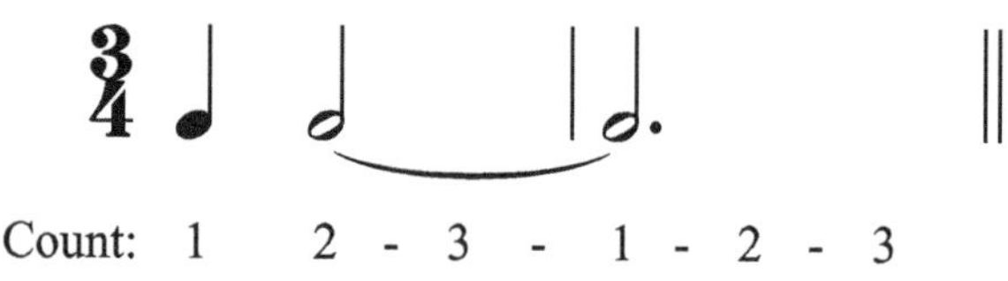

Beautiful Brown Eyes

F: 1ST FRET, 1ST STRING

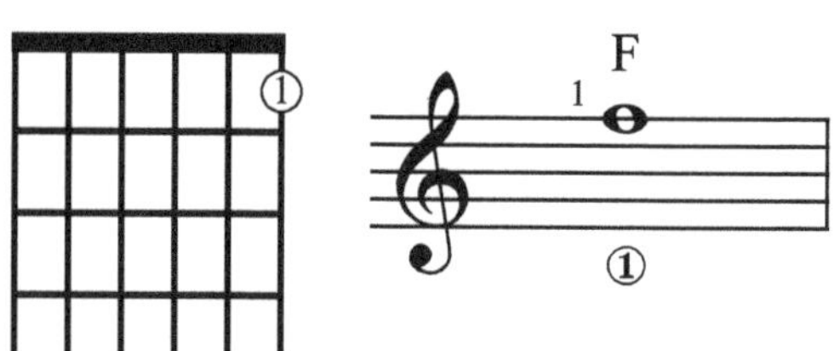

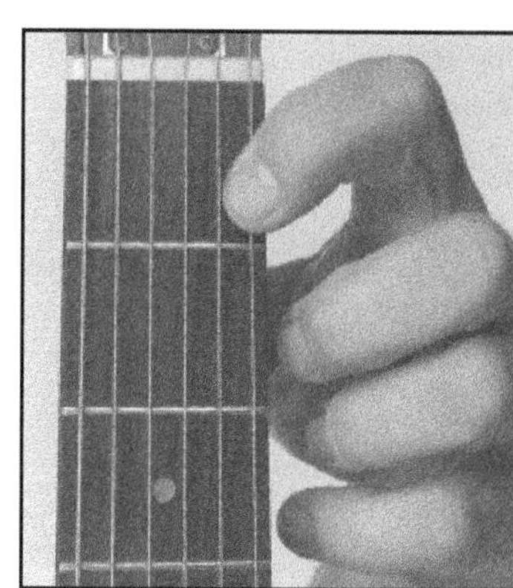

Place the 1st finger of the fretting hand on the 1st fret, as close as possible to the fret wire. The fleshy part of the finger should actually touch the fret wire. In music notation, the F is located on the fifth line of the music staff.

Plaisir d'Amour

(The Joy of Love)

Martini

Quarter Rest

A *rest* is a symbol used in music to indicate silence. For each type of note, there is a rest with the same name and time value. A quarter rest receives one beat.

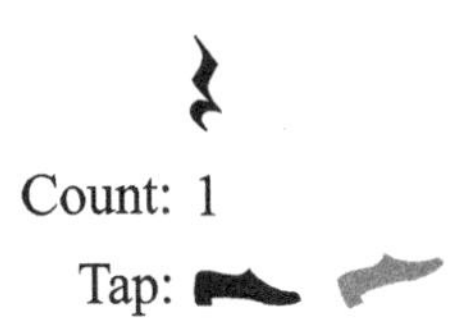

Dynamic Signs

Dynamic signs tell you how loud or soft to play the music. These are signs of musical expression.

p = *piano* (soft)

mp = *mezzo piano* (medium soft))

mf = *mezzo forte* (medium loud)

f = *forte* (loud)

Symphony No. 1

Theme, Fourth Movement (melody)

Johannes Brahms

Combine "Symphony No. 1," example 40, with example 66 (bass part) on page 86.

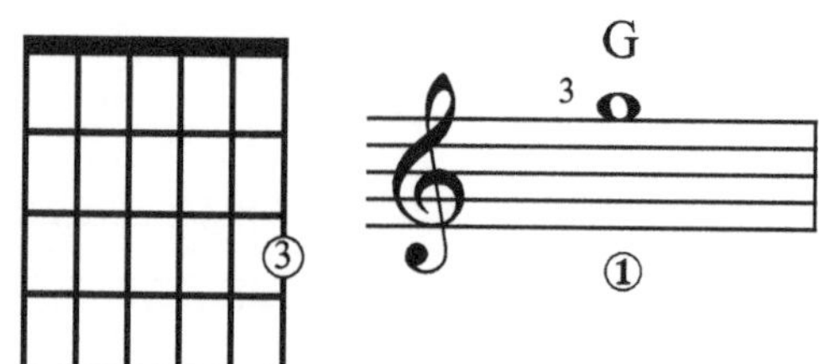

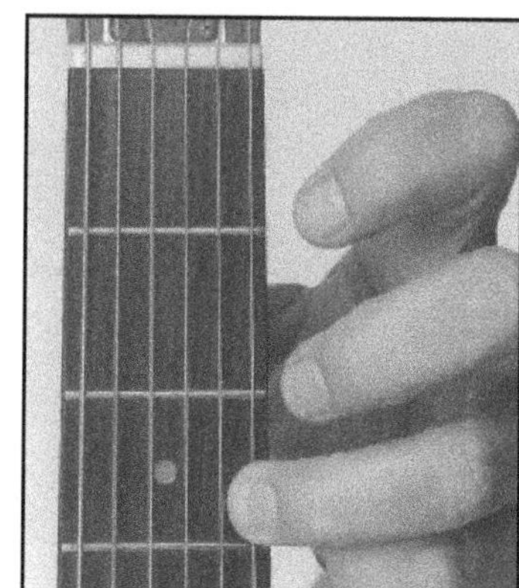

Place the 3rd finger on the 3rd fret, 1st string. Keep the fretting hand fingers spread apart so that the index and middle fingers are over the fingerboard. In music notation, the G is located on the 1st space above the staff.

Ode to Joy

Theme from Symphony No. 9 (melody)

Ludwig van Beethoven

"Ode to Joy," example 43, may be combined with example 62 (bass) on page 85, example 67 (alto) on page 86, and example 84 on page 93.

Andante

(melody)

Fernando Sor

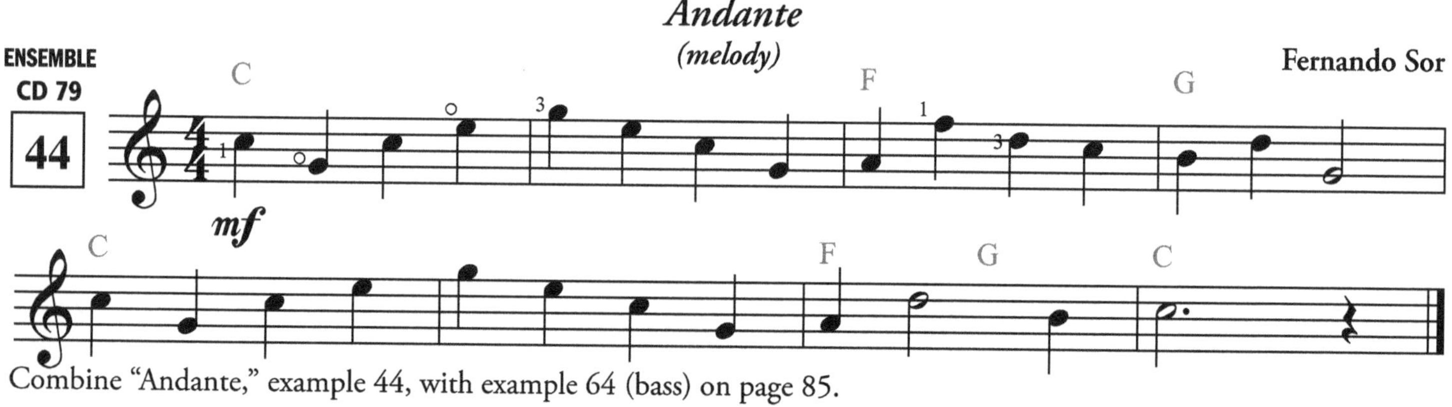

Combine "Andante," example 44, with example 64 (bass) on page 85.

Tempo Markings

Tempo refers to the speed of the music. Various markings are used in music to indicate the tempo.

Largo = slow and broad
Andante = slow and even
Moderato = a moderate tempo
Allegro = fast, quick
Vivace = lively, animated

BASS STRINGS

The 4th, 5th, and 6th strings are the bass strings. In order to notate the bass notes, *ledger lines,* which extend the staff, must be added below the staff. In pickstyle, pluck the bass strings with a down-stroke. In fingerstyle, pluck the notes on these strings with the thumb (*p*) using a free stroke.

G: 3RD FRET, 6TH STRING

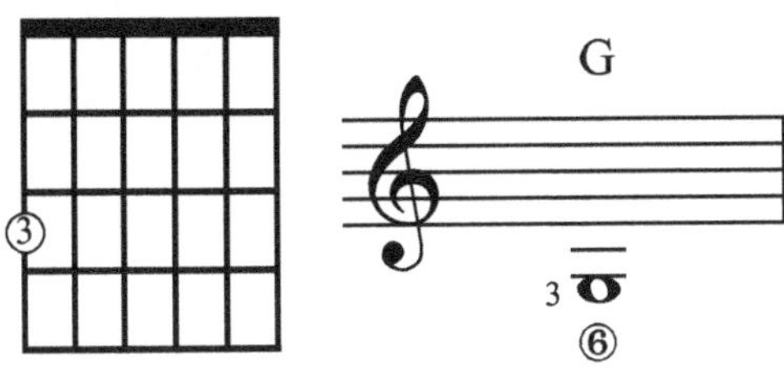

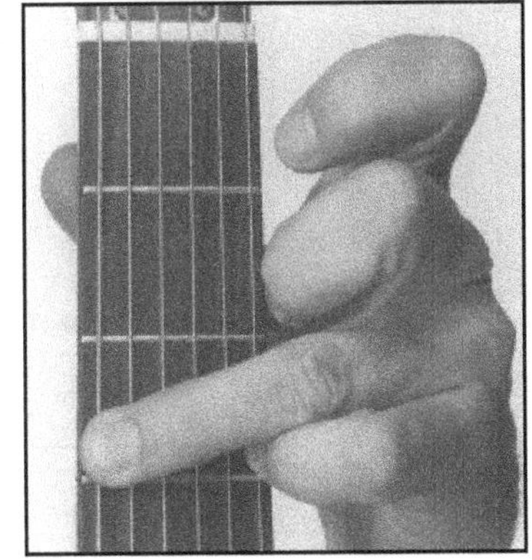

Place the 3rd finger of the fretting hand on the 3rd fret, 6th string. The wrist should be straight, and the palm of the hand should not touch the neck.

CD 80.1

45

A: OPEN, 5TH STRING

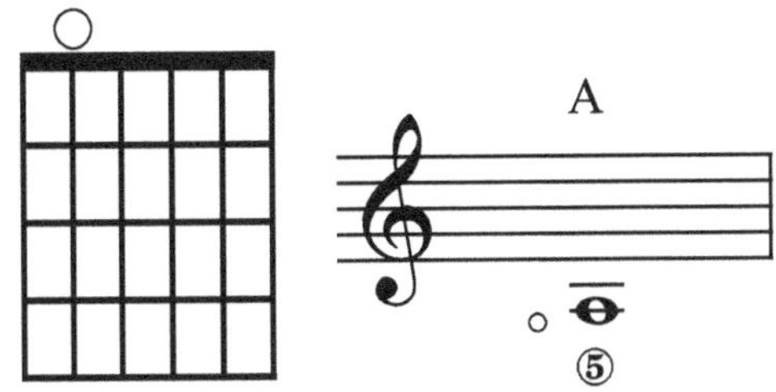

The open 5th string is tuned to A. The A is located on the second ledger line below the staff. Ledger lines are simply an extension of the musical staff.

Ned's Blues

(bass)

Combine "Ned's Blues," example 48, with example 31 (melody) on page 77.

B: 2ND FRET, 5TH STRING

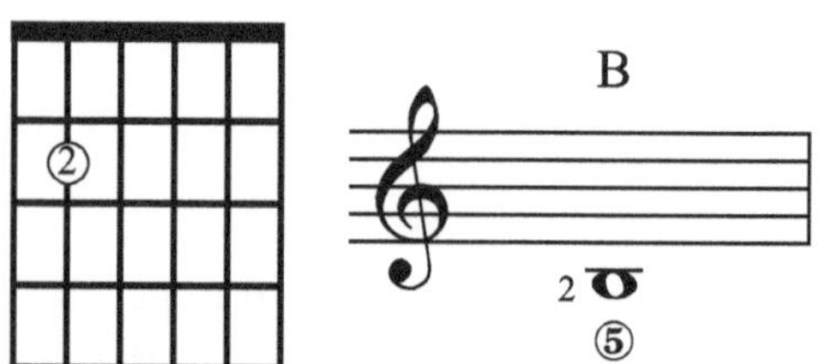

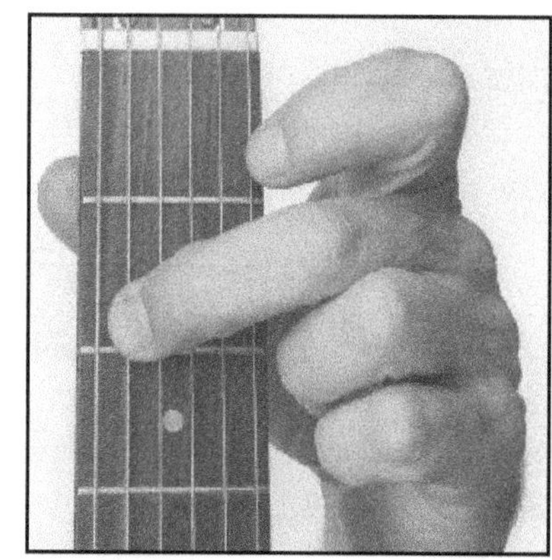

Place the 2nd finger of the fretting hand on the 2nd fret, 5th string. In music notation, the B is located on the space below the first ledger line.

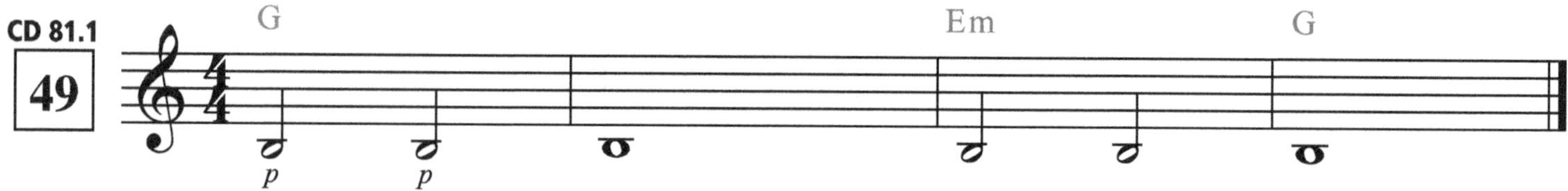

At Pierrot's Door

Traditional

C: 3RD FRET, 5TH STRING

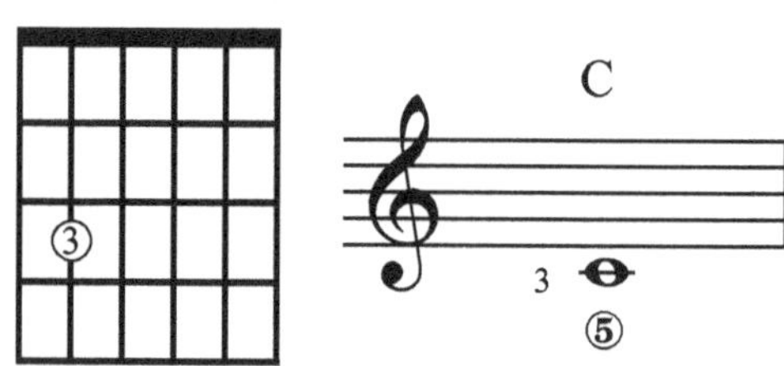

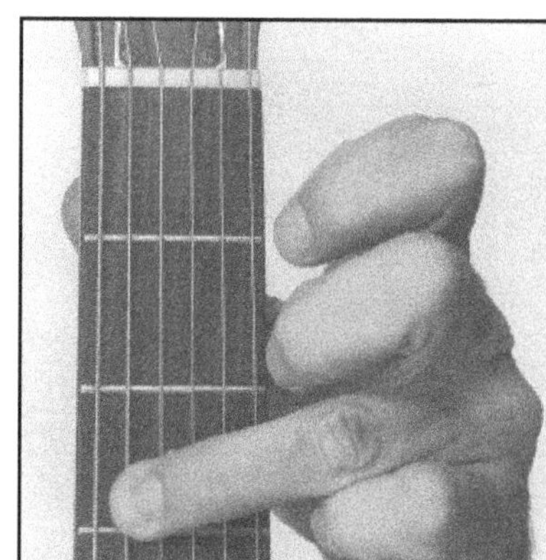

Place the 3rd finger of the fretting hand on the 3rd fret, 5th string. In music notation, the C is located on the first ledger line below the staff.

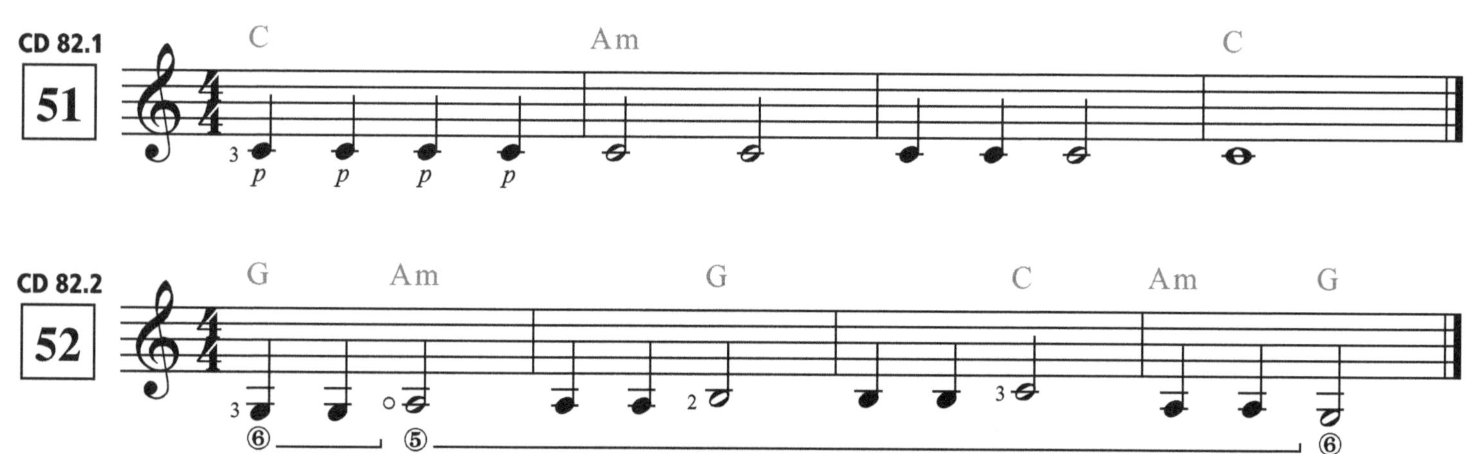

Marianne

(trio)

ENSEMBLE
CD 83
53

Traditional

Moderately, with a beat

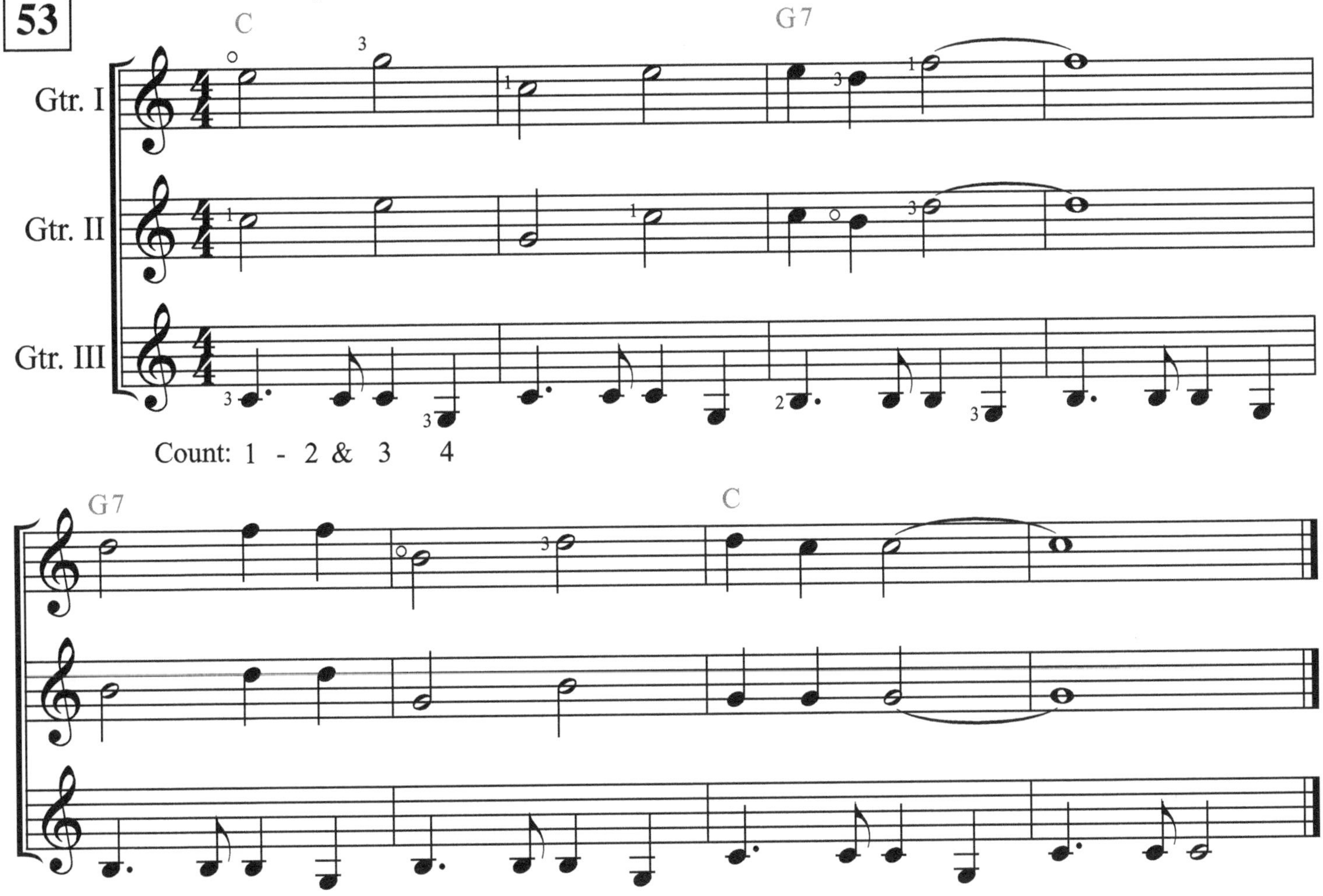
C
G7
Gtr. I
Gtr. II
Gtr. III
Count: 1 - 2 & 3 4
G7
C

D: OPEN, 4TH STRING

D
④

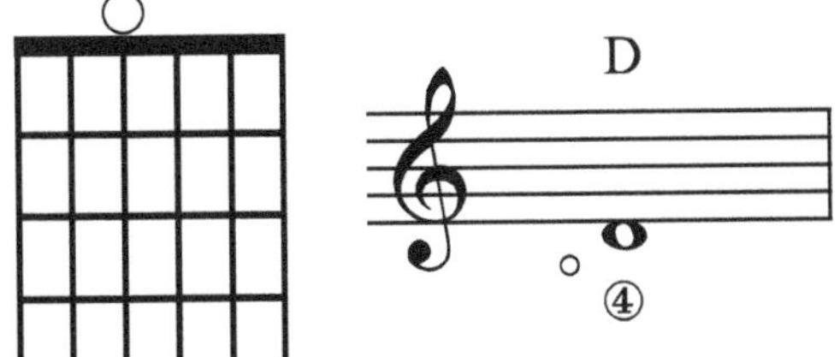

The open 4th string is tuned to D. In music notation, the D is located on the first space below the music staff.

CD 84.1
54

D
G
D
p p p p p

CD 84.2
55

G
D7
G
D7
G
⑥ ⑤ ④ ⑤ ⑥ ⑤ ④ ⑥

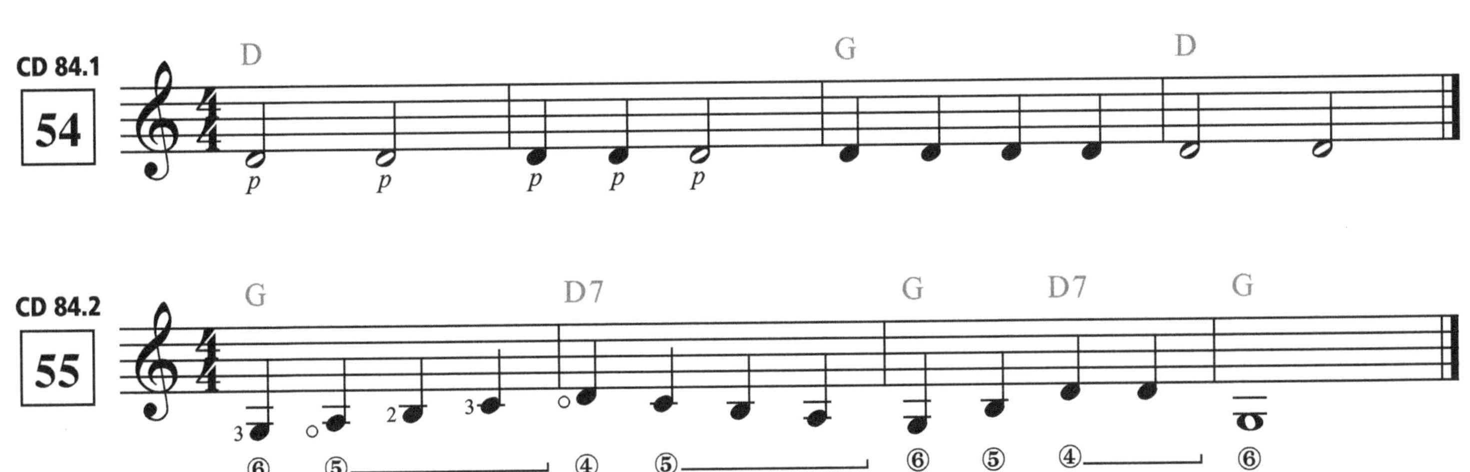

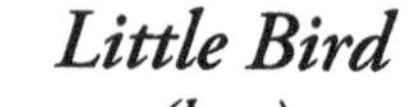

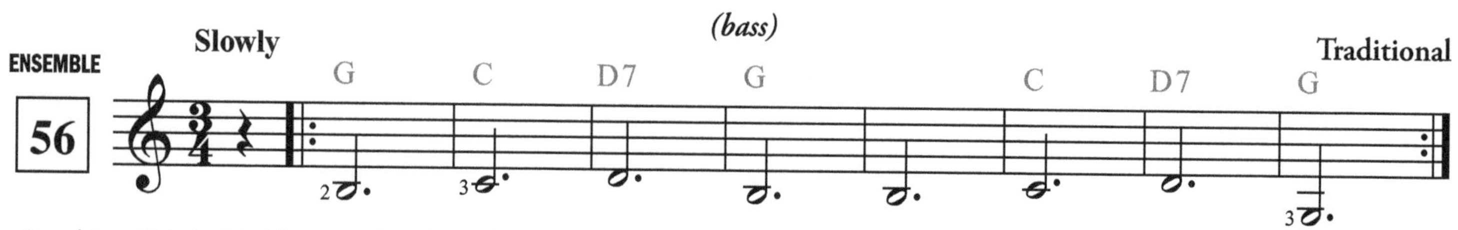

Combine "Little Bird," example 56, with example 26 (melody) on page 75.

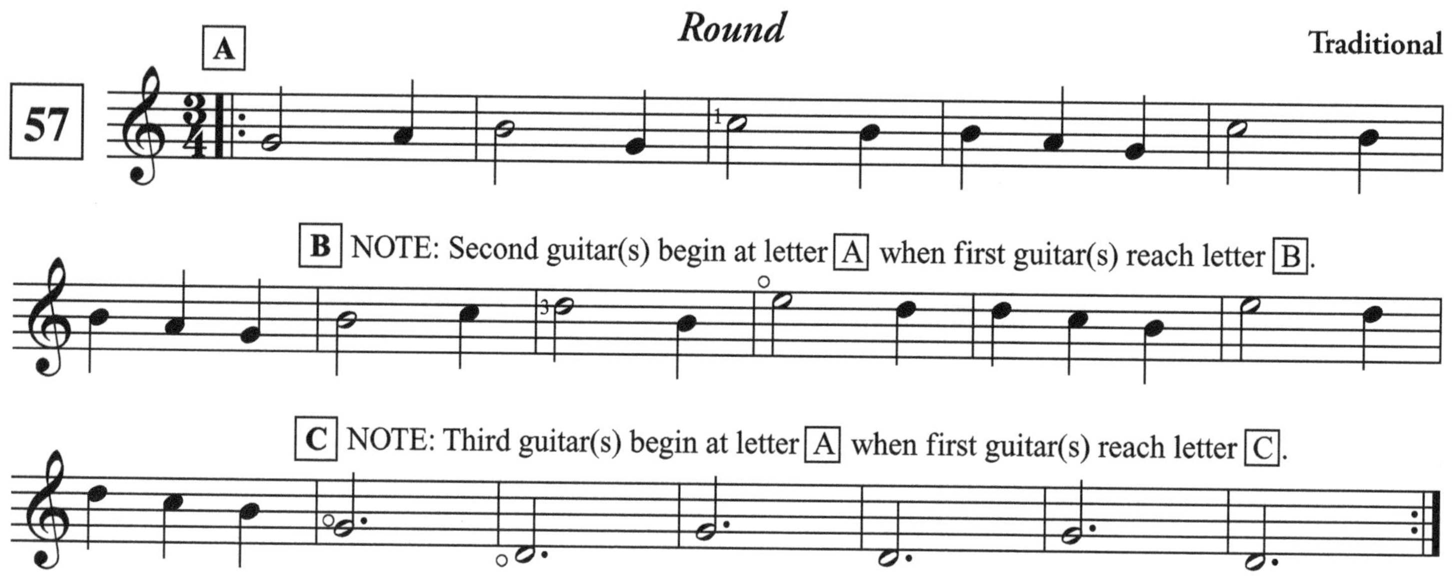

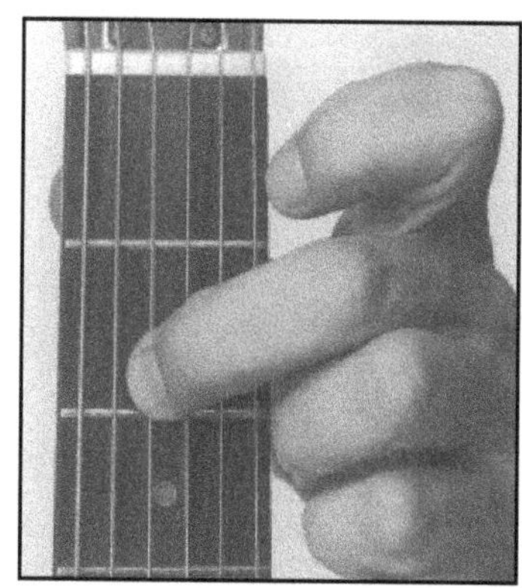

Place the 2nd finger on the 2nd fret, 4th string. The E is located on the first line of the music staff.

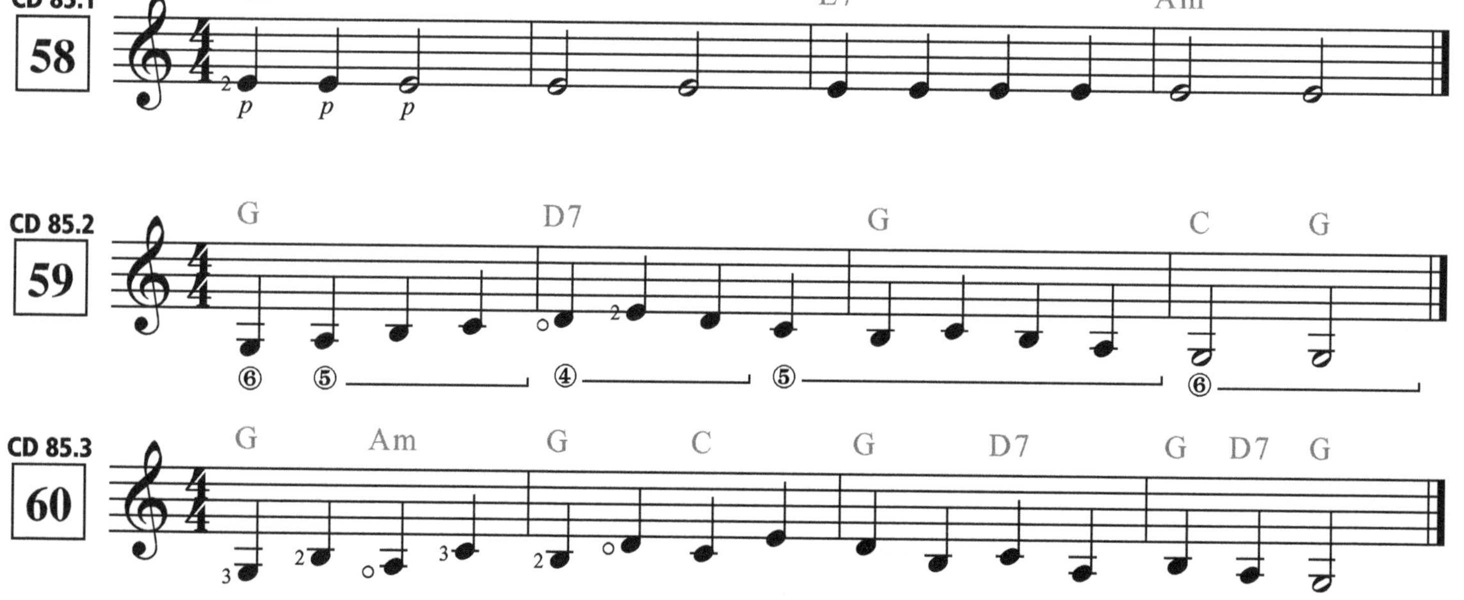

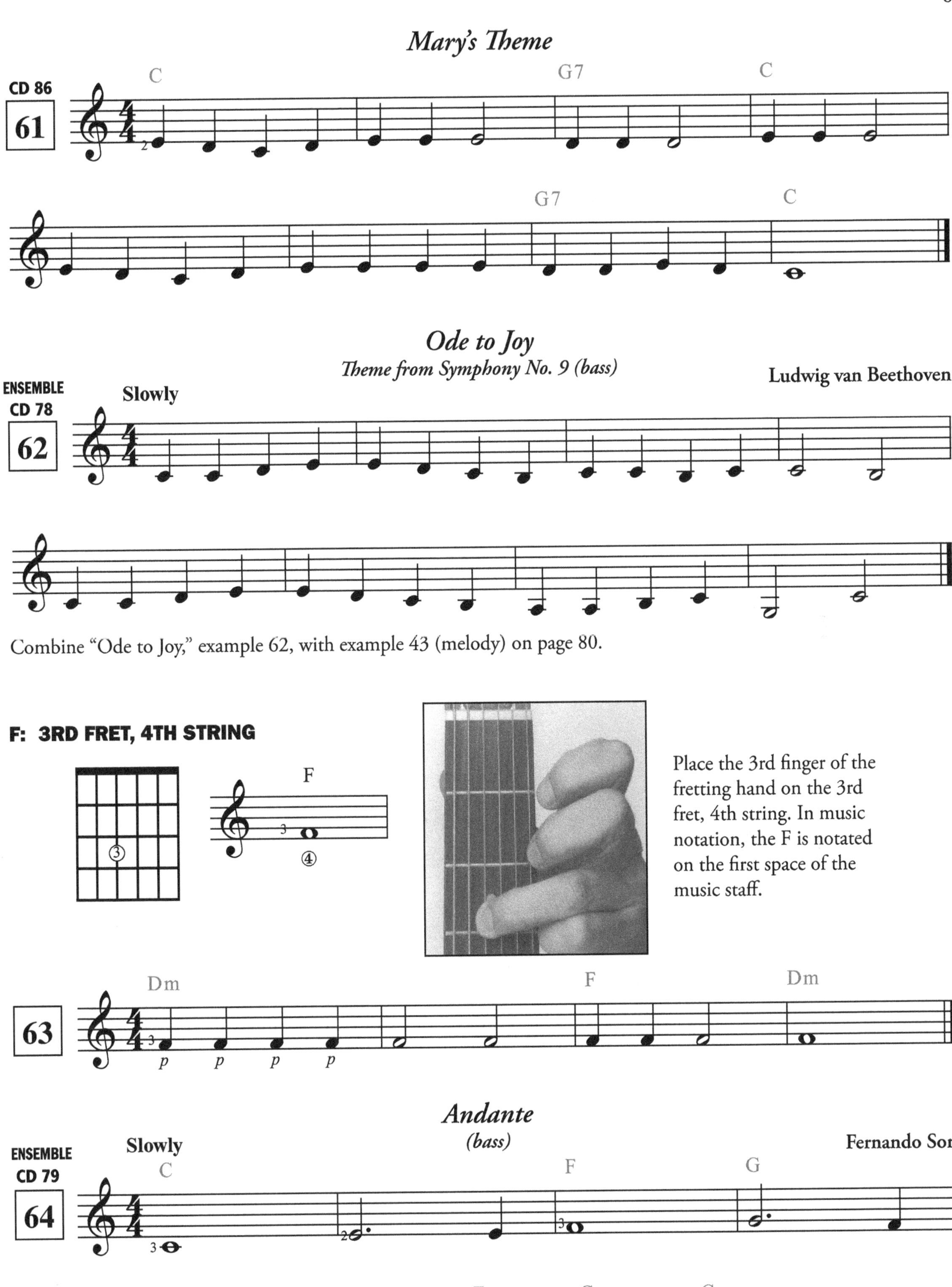

Combine "Andante," example 64 with example 44 (melody) on page 80.

Old Joe Clark

Traditional

Symphony No. 1

Theme, Fourth Movement (bass)

Johannes Brahms

Combine "Symphony No. 1," example 66 (bass), with example 40 (melody) on page 79.

Ode to Joy

(alto)

Ludwig van Beethoven

Combine "Ode to Joy," example 67, with example 43 (melody) on page 80 and example 62 (bass) on page 85.

Fermata

A *fermata* is a hold, or pause sign that indicates a note should be held or sustained longer than its normal duration.

𝄐 = fermata (hold)

First and Second Endings

Quite often music repeats itself. *First and second endings* are used to save space.

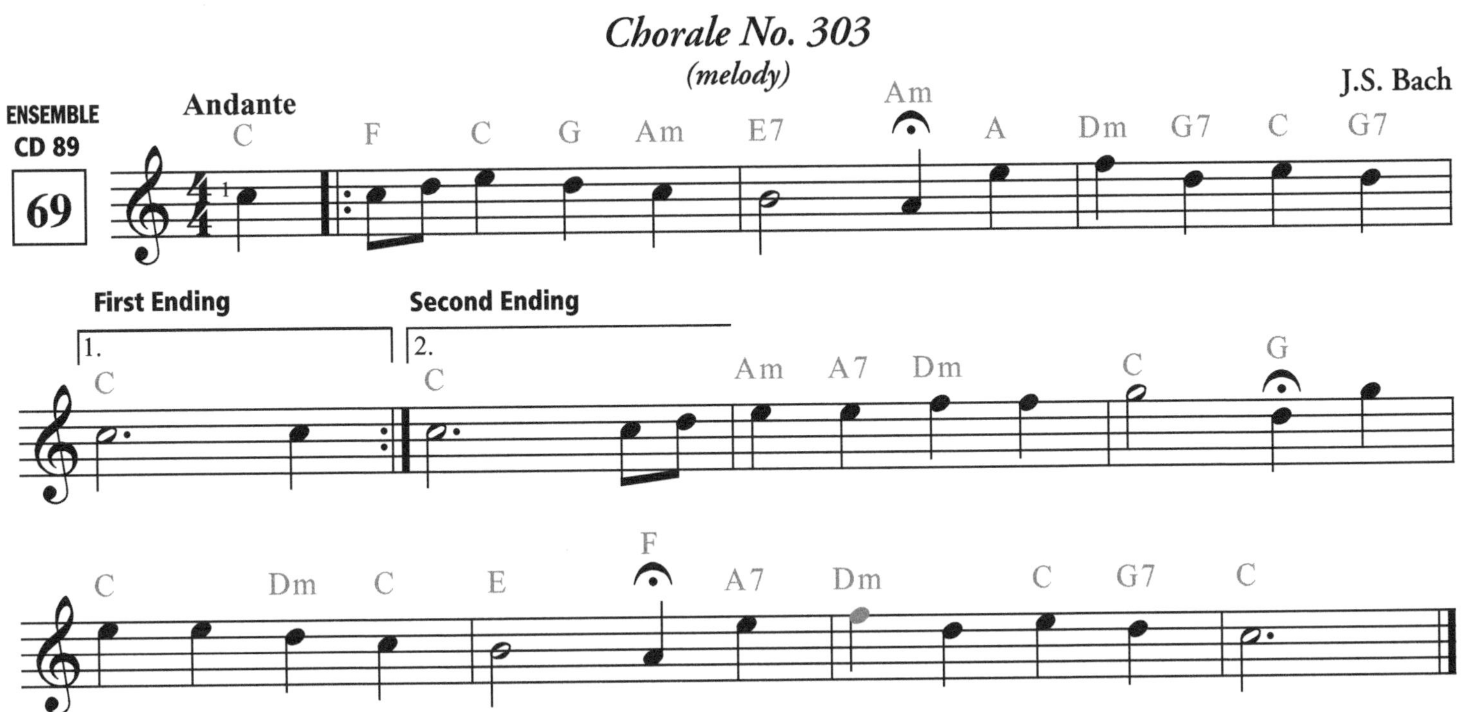

"Chorale No. 303," example 69 (melody) may be combined with example 82 (bass) on page 91.

Sharps and Naturals

A *sharp* place before a note indicates to play the note one half step higher. On the guitar, that is the distance of one fret. A *natural* sign is used to cancel the effect of a sharp. A bar line cancels all sharps and naturals preceding it.

♯ = a **sharp** raises the tone 1/2 step upward

♮ = a **natural** sign cancels the sharp

F♯: 2ND FRET, 1ST STRING

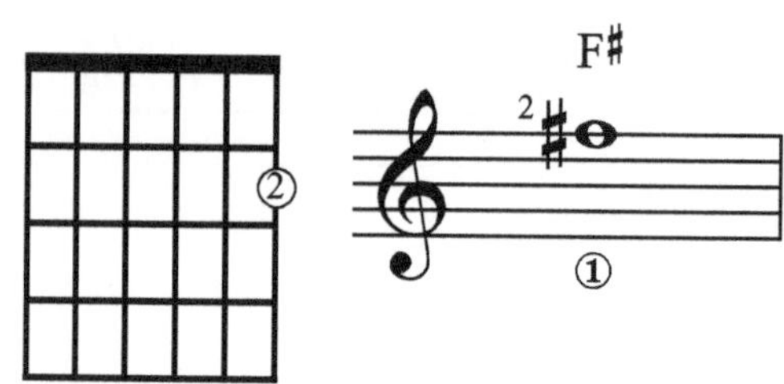

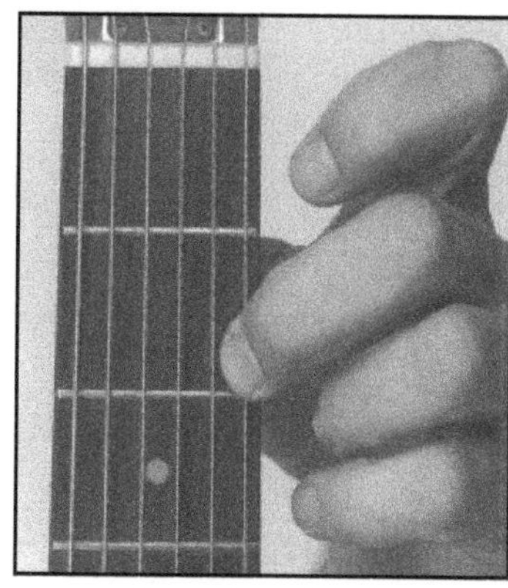

Place the 2nd finger of the fretting hand on the 2nd fret, 1st string. Place the finger right behind the fret wire. The palm of the hand should not touch the neck of the guitar.

Anonymous

Moderately

G Major Scale

The *major* scale is the most commonly used scale. It is a series of eight successive tones that have a defined pattern of whole and half steps. The scale provides the skeleton upon which the melody of the song is based. The G major scale begins and ends on G.

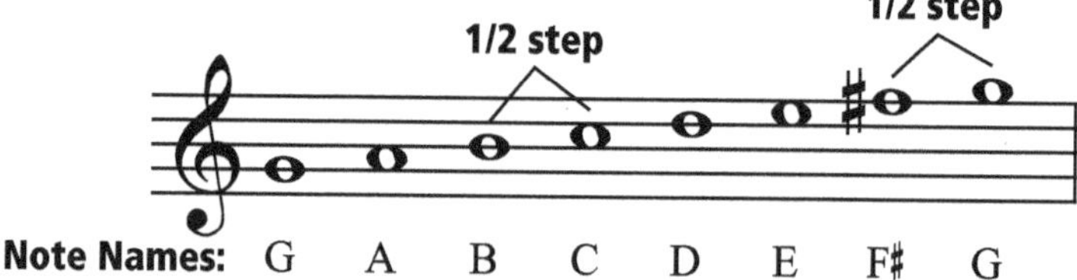

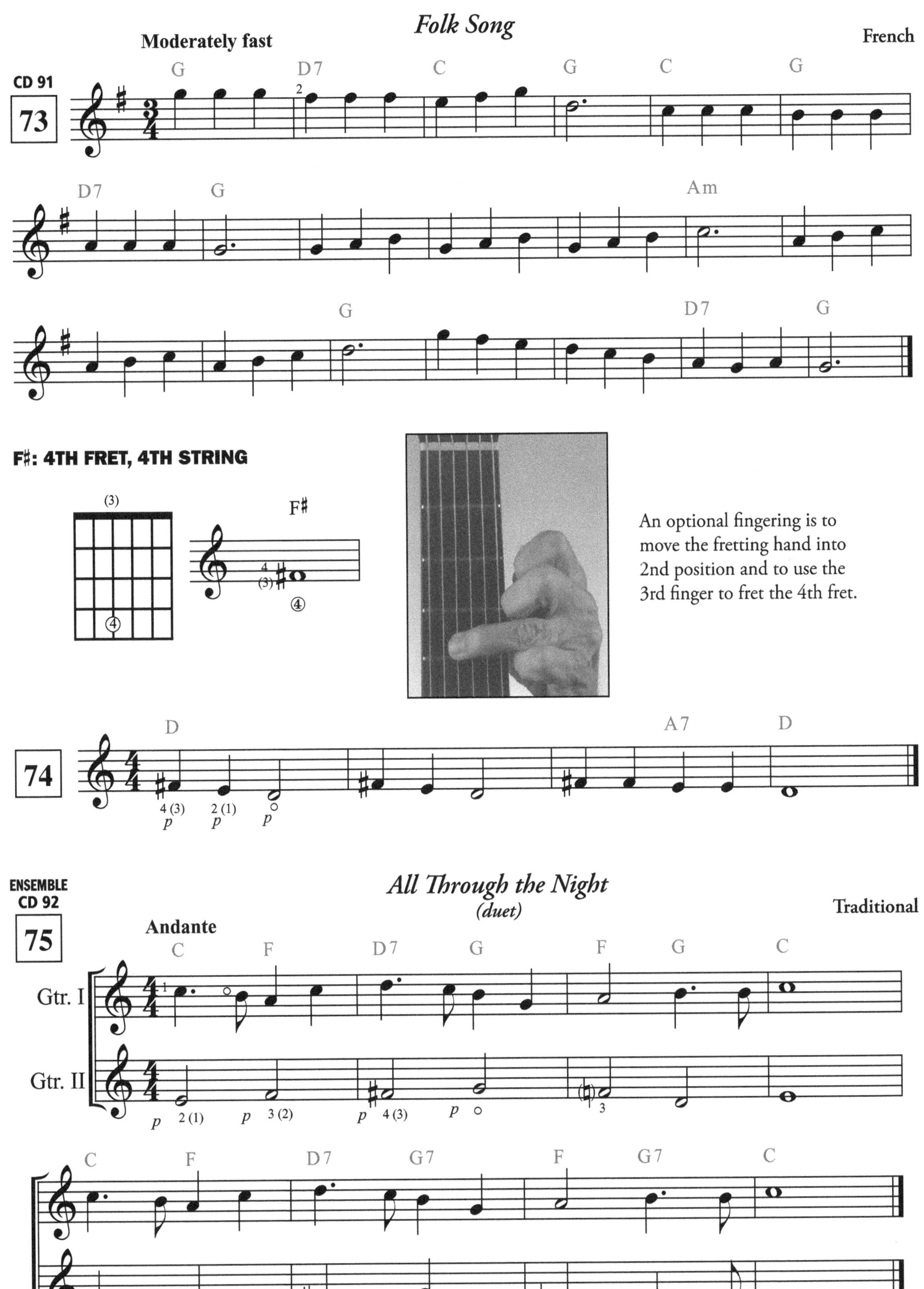
Folk Song
Moderately fast
French
CD 91
73
G D7 C G C G
D7 G Am
G D7 G
F♯: 4TH FRET, 4TH STRING
(3)
F♯
An optional fingering is to move the fretting hand into 2nd position and to use the 3rd finger to fret the 4th fret.
74
D A7 D
ENSEMBLE
CD 92
75
All Through the Night
(duet)
Traditional
Andante
C F D7 G F G C
Gtr. I
Gtr. II
C F D7 G7 F G7 C

E & F♯: OPEN & 2ND FRET, 6TH STRING

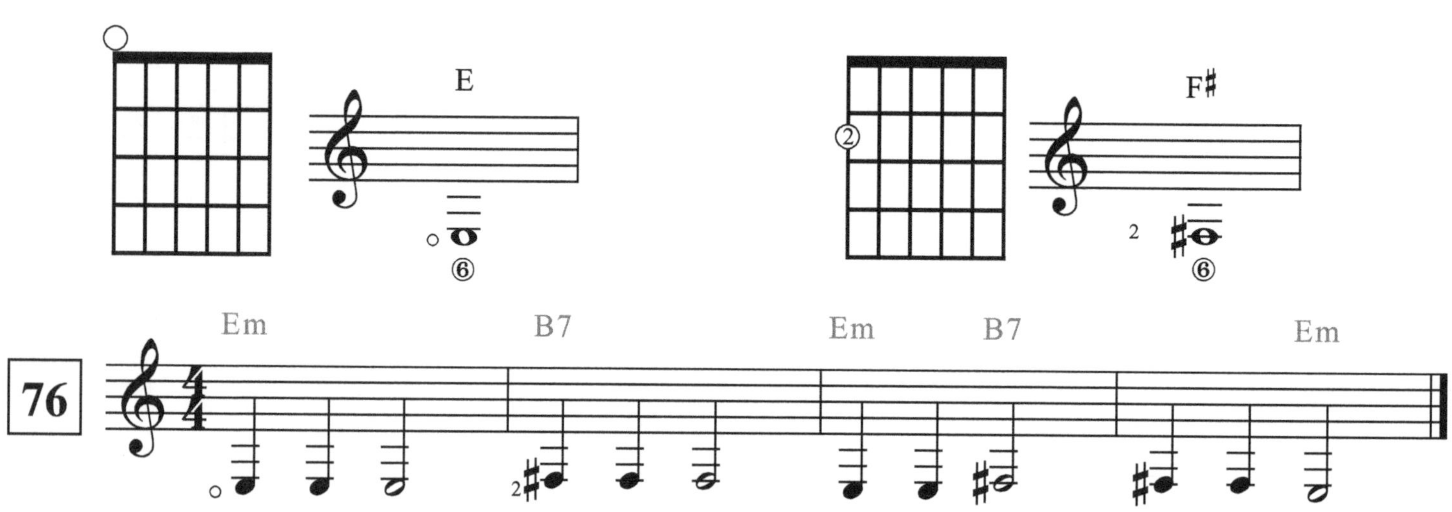

ENSEMBLE
CD 64

Jesu, Joy of Man's Desiring

(alto & bass)

J.S. Bach

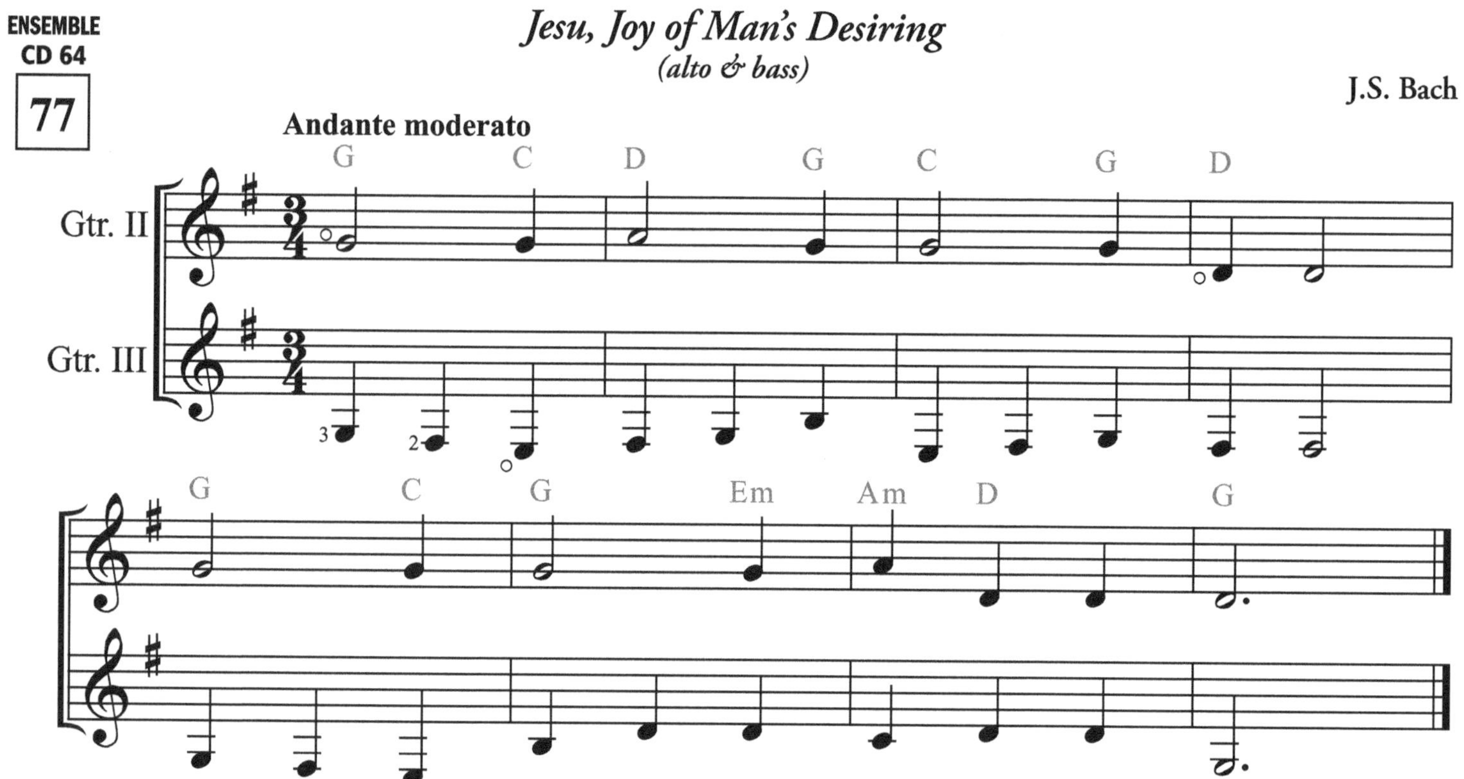

Combine "Jesu, Joy of Man's Desiring," example 77, with example 20 (melody) on page 73.

G Scale, Two Octaves

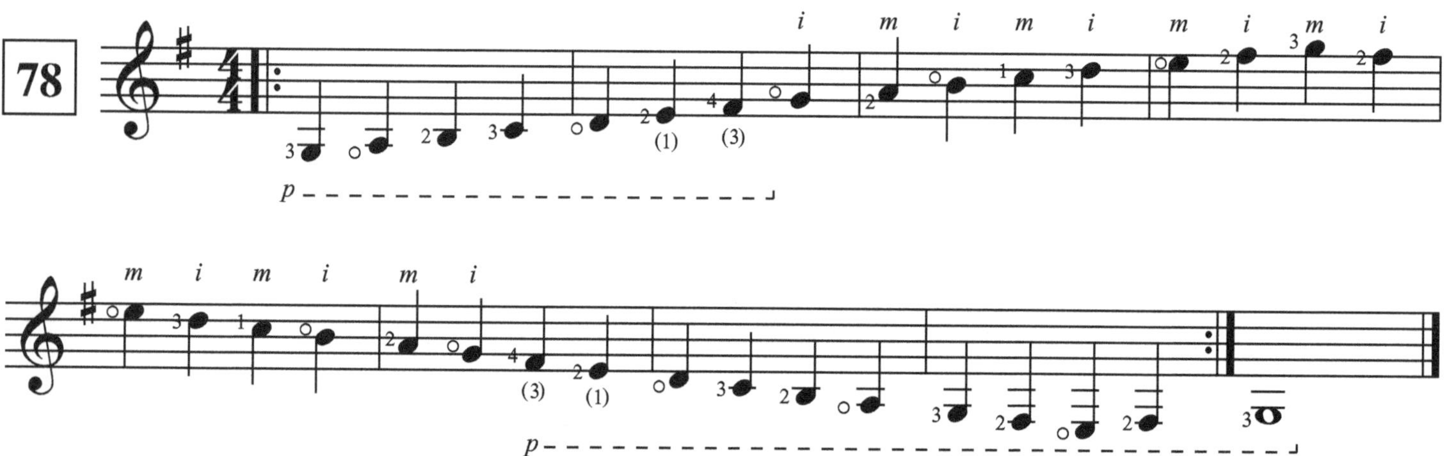

More Sharps

Examples 79 and 80 may be played together.

CD 93.1

79

G
G♯
A
A♯
C
C♯
D
D♯

CD 93.2

80

G
G♯
A
A♯
C
C♯
D
D♯

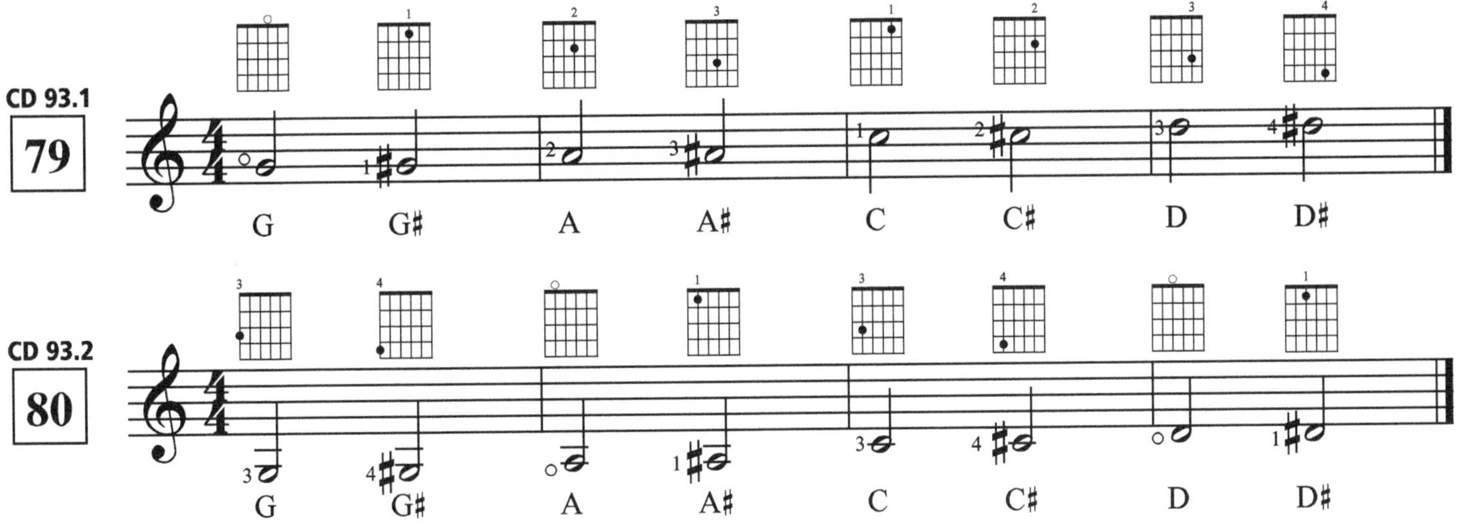

Chromatic Scale

A *chromatic scale* is a scale in which each successive note is a *half step* apart. In music notation, sharps are generally used in the **ascending** chromatic scale. The following study is a two-octave chromatic scale on G. Memorize this scale and use it as a warm-up exercise. In fingerstyle, play the bass notes with the thumb (free strokes) and the treble strings with alternating index and middle fingers (rest strokes). In pickstyle, use down-strokes with a pick.

CD 93.3

81

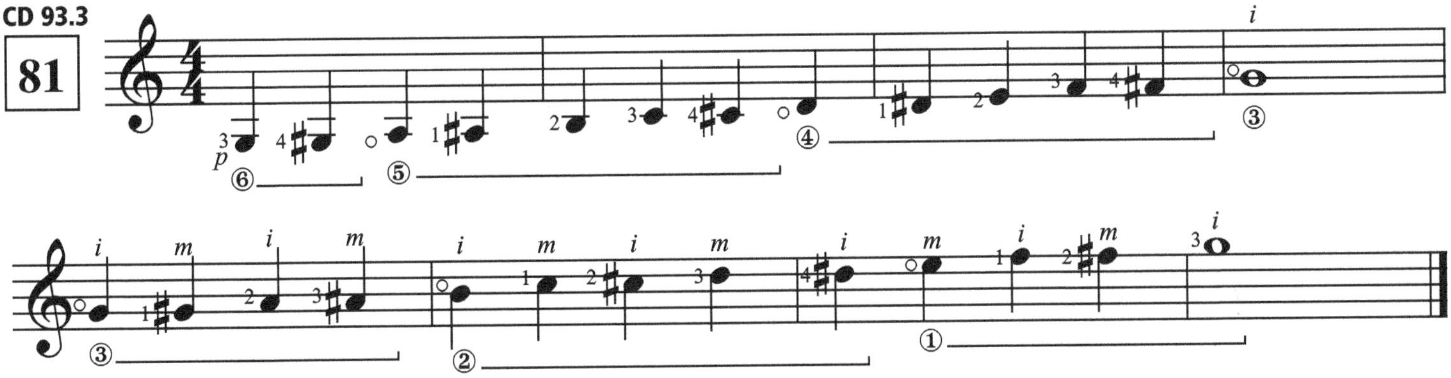

Chorale No. 303

(bass)

J.S. Bach

ENSEMBLE
CD 89

82

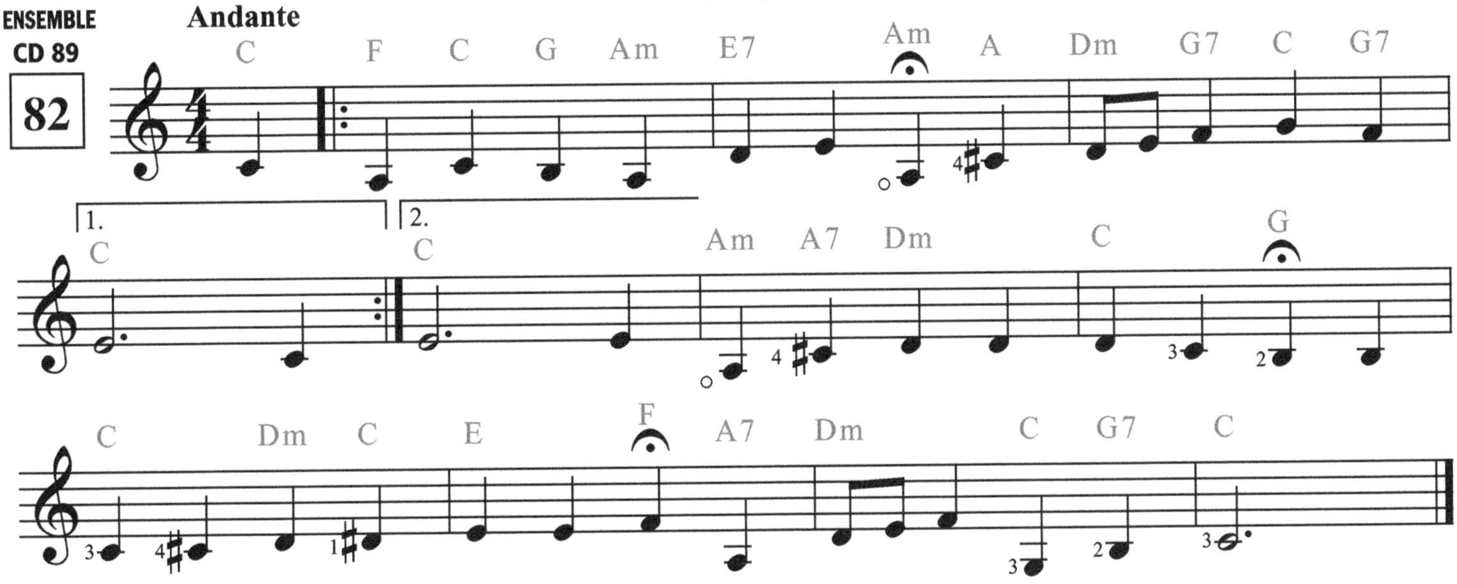

Andante
C
F
C
G
Am
E7
Am
A
Dm
G7
C
G7
1.
C
2.
C
Am
A7
Dm
C
G
C
Dm
C
E
F
A7
Dm
C
G7
C

Combine "Chorale No. 303," example 82, with example 69 (melody) on page 87.

Greensleeves

What Child Is This? (duet)

ENSEMBLE
CD 94

83

Ode to Joy

(optional part)

Ludwig van Beethoven

Combine "Ode to Joy," example 84, with examples 43 (melody) on page 80, 62 (bass) on page 85, and 67 (alto) on page 86 for a quartet.

ENSEMBLE
CD 95

85

Bourree

(duet)

J.S. Bach

Gtr. I

Gtr. II

*Note: Alternate fingerings are indicated in parentheses.

A: 5TH FRET, 1ST STRING

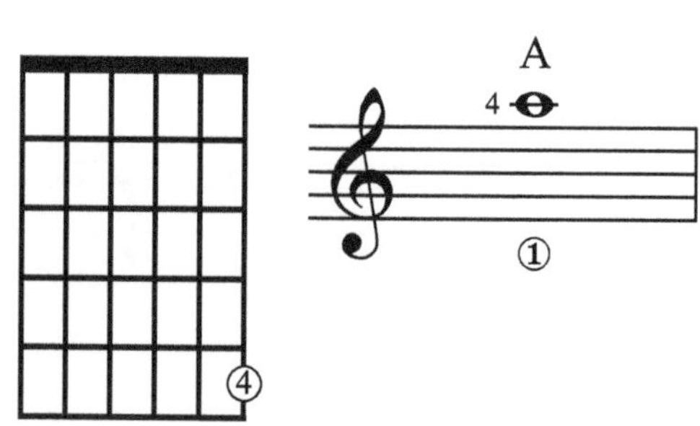

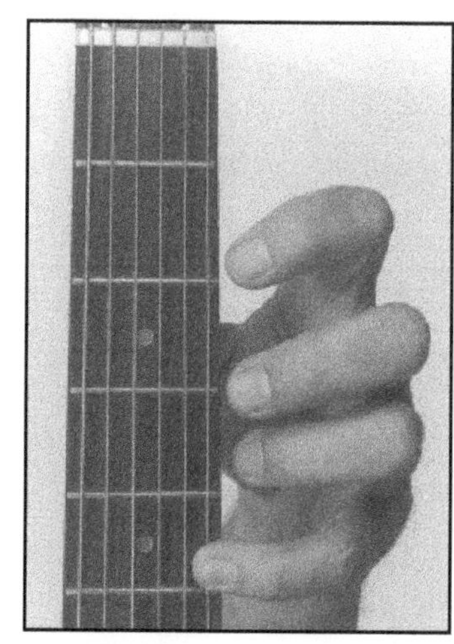

Move your fretting hand into the 2nd position; your 1st finger is now over the 2nd fret so that you can reach the 5th fret with your 4th finger. In music notation, the A is located on the first ledger line above the music staff

ENSEMBLE
CD 96

86

Du, Du Liegst Mir Im Herzen

You Live in My Heart (duet)

German Folk Song

ENSEMBLE
CD 97

87

House of the Rising Sun

(trio)

Traditional

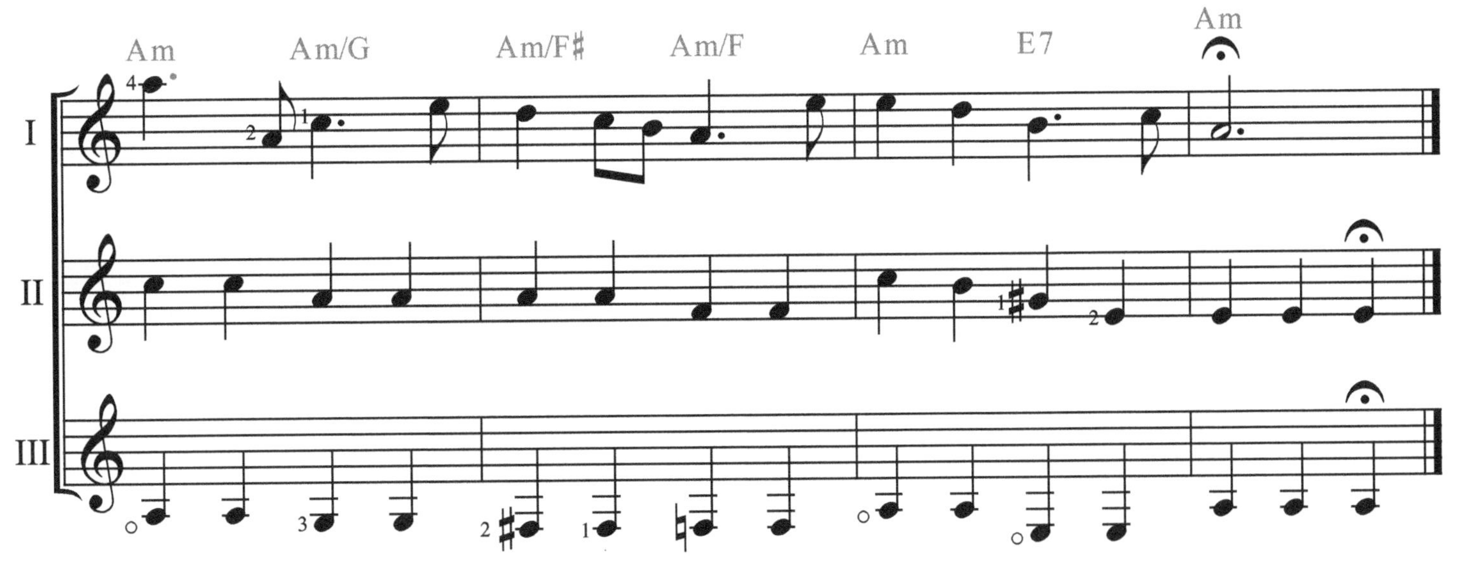

Am
Am/G
Am/F♯
Am/F
Am
E7
Am
I
II
III

Now the Day Is Over

(trio)

ENSEMBLE
CD 98

88

Joseph Barnby

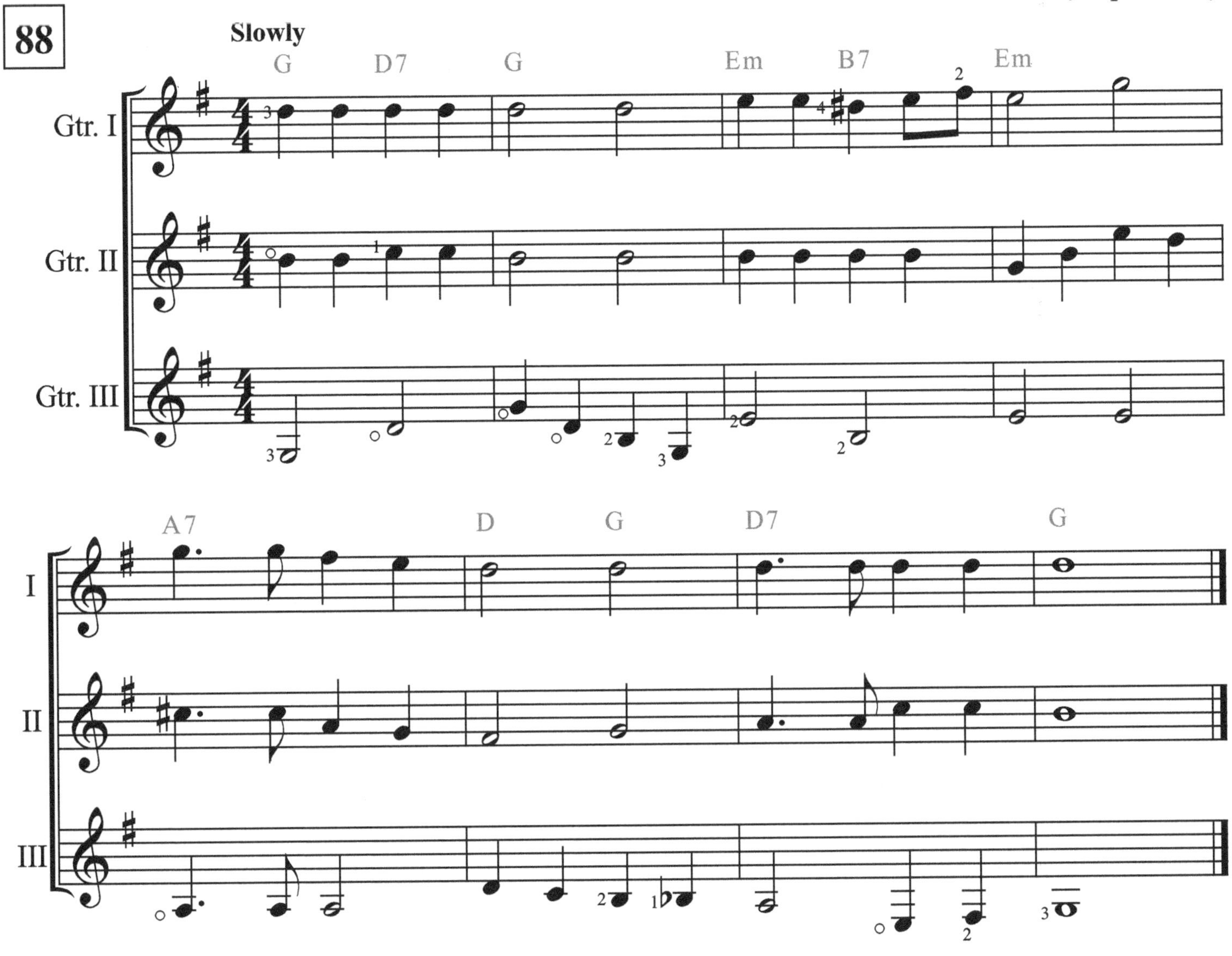
Slowly
G
D7
G
Em
B7
Em
Gtr. I
Gtr. II
Gtr. III
A7
D
G
D7
G
I
II
III

Scarborough Fair

(trio)

ENSEMBLE
CD 99

89

Traditional